The Art of Scale Weaving

(A new look into the relationships between triads, pentatonic scales, and heptatonic scales.)

Juan Antonio Rivera

Violet Anamnesis Publications

San Diego, California

Violet Anamnesis Publications
11880 Bernardo Terrace Suite B
San Diego, California /92128

The Art of Scale Weaving / Juan Antonio Rivera —1st Ed.
ISBN 978-1-944213-40-4

Table of Contents

Chapter Two: Melodic Minor Scale and Modes 70

Chapter Three: Harmonic Minor Scale and Modes 125

Dedication

To everyone and anyone looking for their own way;

I truly hope you find it.

Thank You

Family:

Violeta González Bonilla (mom): for teaching me kindness, love, hard work, and an infinite amount of lessons in life and beyond. Love you always!

Wilson Rivera Ramos (dad): for your unconditional support, love and teaching me to carry on no matter what. Love You!

Jan Rivera: for providing a road to follow throughout the first steps of my musical journey and for pushing me to create this book while providing the space and resources to make it possible.

Francisca "Panchita" Castro: for your constant support, humility, unconditional love and always believing in me.

And the rest of my family: Andrés Rivera, Armando Rivera, Alba Nydia Rivera and Efrén Rivera.

Friends/Co-workers:

Pierre Bou: for a lifelong friendship/brotherhood through good times and bad.

Misa 'E Gallo: for providing a creative space full of love, music, growth and incredible musical experiences.

Franko Torres: for pushing me to work more when I was feeling lazy, for the late night calls while constantly driving and for helping out in tough emotional times.

CAC: Rubén and the family at the Conservatorio de Artes del Caribe for providing a home to work in and creating the perfect educational atmosphere to create musical interest in young musicians (thus, creating the need to communicate these ideas with my students).

Girlfriend:

Enidza Samot Feliciano: for your kindness, your love, your positivity, your tolerance, your company and the constant support in the creation of the book.

Teachers:

Alex Machacek: for teaching me one of the most important lessons that I've learned in life; how to learn.

Chris Juergensen: for demystifying the instrument; making it easy and fun while the rest of the world was trying to make it seem more complicated.

Students:

In general: for providing the necessity to create such a system of connection; without their need for understanding this book would have probably never happened.

I truly love you all!

Preface

There is but one purpose for this book; and that purpose is connection. It is through connection that we broaden our spectrum of understanding of the language of music. It is within the tightly woven relationships that appear between different musical concepts that I have grown in my own musical journey. I have used these relationships to help others in their journey and have seen many musicians blossom with these same ideas of connection. Now I am nothing more than hopeful that the ideas within this book will help carry the message of musical connection to you.

Once absorbed, the concepts within this book should be personalized by your own artistic take. The concepts within these pages are merely palates of colors waiting to be used on your musical canvas. As such these must be learned, applied and customized to your liking. Without your artistic vision as an engine of creation, the information in these pages would be pointless.

Prerequisites

Notes on the Fretboard

It is important that you know the notes on the fretboard so that you may use them as a guide when tackling the material in the book. It is much easier to have a clear understanding of what and where before getting to work on the abundance of material that lies within the pages of this book.

Below is a guitar neck diagram with all the natural notes (no accidentals) in display.

*Could also be seen as the C major scale all over the fretboard.

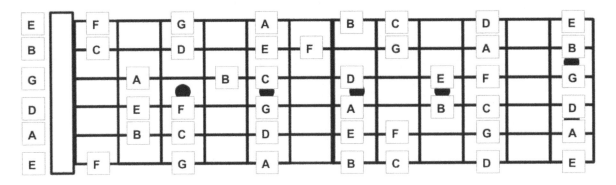

CAGED System and its octaves

The CAGED system originates from the use of five main open position chords and their root positioning. These five chords (as the name spells) are the C chord, A chord, G chord, E chord and D chord. The roots of these five chords are placed in such a way that they perfectly divide the neck of the instrument into five separately positioned octaves when remaining in one key.

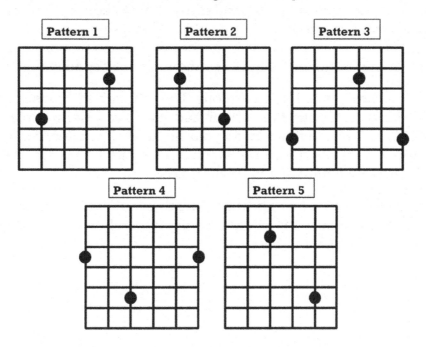

This comes in handy when trying to learn a scale, arpeggio or different voicings of a chord all over the fretboard. Below is a fretboard diagram displaying the five positions of the CAGED system when using the note C as the root.

- Example over C root

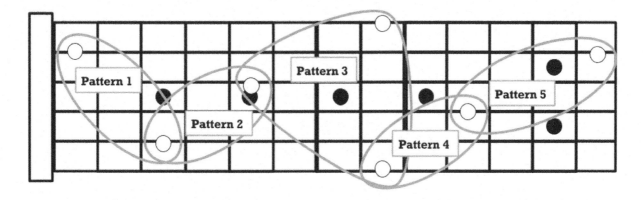

Basic harmony and theory knowledge

To understand the material within the book; you should have a grasp on the theory behind note names, intervals, scale construction, chord construction, chord scales, etc. (even though you can find some quick explanations to some of these concepts within the book).

It's also important to know what the modes are, how to construct them, over which chords they work and how they relate to their parent scale. Most of the information in this book deals with the core scales in music (major, melodic minor, harmonic minor and harmonic major) and their seven respective modes.

You should also know some basic harmony. Even though the construction of triads, chords, chord scales and the harmonized scale are briefly explained in the book; it's highly suggested that you do your homework and learn a bit of harmony. The application of the material in the book could be hindered if you don't have a solid harmony foundation to relate it to.

You don't really have to be an expert on the subject of harmony and theory to get results from the diagrams in the book; but you definitely need a good grasp on the topic to get the most out the book.

Introduction

The material in this book is divided into four chapters. Each chapter deals with a different scale with a set three of subtopics (except for the major scale which deals with four subtopics). The four scales worked in the book are the major scale, the melodic minor scale, the harmonic minor scale and the harmonic major scale.

These are the subtopics within each of the chapters:

- Scale Packs

The idea behind the scale packs came from a CAGED system packet of triads, pentatonic scales, major/minor scales, chords and octave shapes that I hand out to just about all of my students in class. I've always seen it as some of the core essentials that every guitarist should know.

I then modified it into a trio of triad, pentatonic scale and heptatonic scale diagrams to be played from the same root. The idea is to create a relationship between all 3 concepts; to make them as interchangeable as possible in the mind of the student.

In my classes I usually start with the major and minor scale packs, but for the purposes of the book, I decided to expand the concept into all seven modes of the major, melodic minor, harmonic minor and harmonic major scales.

- Harmonized Scale Weaving

The idea behind the harmonized scale weaving concept came from two different sources. The first being a jazz guitar course that I took in college with a professor named Joe Elliot in which we would play all the 7th arpeggios in a jazz standard over just one position of the CAGED system. This facilitates the process of finding the chord tones in a tune while improvising.

The other source of inspiration for this concept came from my private instructor at college Alex Machacek, who would make me adapt any type of phrasing pattern to each and every note of whichever scale I was using, in a horizontal fashion. This made me think of the same phrase as it adapted to the seven modes of the scale and I would have to move the root along the same string.

The actual harmonized scale weaving concept is a mixture of both ideas. It's the application of the harmonized scale in the form of 7th arpeggios in two different ways.

The first application is called Vertical Harmonized Scale Weaving and in this case you just play the harmonized scale in the form of 7th arpeggios in just one position of the CAGED system. Once this is done, you move to the next and so on until you play all five patterns of the CAGED system.

The second application is called Horizontal Harmonized Scale Weaving and in this case you play the harmonized scale in the form of 7th arpeggios with the different roots all played over just one string. This results in a position shift for most of the arpeggios to be played.

With these exercises comes the concept of scale weaving in which both the arpeggio and parent scale of that arpeggio are displayed simultaneously in just one diagram with a system of color coded dots. As with all concepts in this book, the main idea is one of connection; being able to picture both the arpeggio and heptatonic scale in your mind at the same time.

- Pentatonic Scale Weaving

The next concept is Pentatonic Scale Weaving; the reasoning behind this concept is to unify the visualization of the pentatonic scale and its parent heptatonic scale. This happens by utilizing a pentatonic (5 note) scale as a base and adding 2 more notes to it to obtain a heptatonic scale.

I've heard a lot of different musicians speaking of this type of visualization; especially when talking about infusing a pentatonic vocabulary (such as the blues) with more tones, colors and passages from other scales.

This is where the concept of scale weaving steps in. Pentatonic Scale Weaving (like Harmonized Scale Weaving) uses a system of color coding to display both the pentatonic and heptatonic scales over just one diagram.

- Pentatonic Scale Substitutions (only for the major scale)

Pentatonic Scale Substitutions are not something new; they have been used by the masters for quite some time. I actually learned about this topic from my college professor Alex Machacek. The idea behind this concept is that you can play three completely different pentatonic scales from within one of the modes of the major scale. The reason why this works is that when all 3 of those scales are connected you end up with the seven degrees of that specific mode.

Yet again, I decided to apply the concept of scale weaving over this concept and created a series of diagrams that display both the pentatonic scale (all three substitutions) and the heptatonic scale with the use of color coding.

Chapter One

Major Scale and Modes

The major scale (and its modes) is probably the most used scale in all western music. You can hear it almost instantly when turning on the radio, listening to your albums (online radio now days) and more than probably on your own songs. It is absolutely everywhere and a must when studying music.

The major scale is constructed by a series of whole tones (W) and half tones (H) that when put together looks something like this: W W H W W W H. Most western theory out there is related to the major scale and when spelled out in intervallic terms it looks something like this: 1 2 3 4 5 6 7. So when discussing any other musical concept theory wise, a lot of people just communicate by using the major scale as a base and altering and/or leaving out any number of notes that need be left out.

It is with this intervallic numeration method that I will be explaining most concepts in this book.

The modes are a variety of scales that result from building a heptatonic scale from any one of the scale degrees found in a parent scale (in this case the major scale). This newly chosen scale degree is seen as the root, while the rest of the notes are based on the original construction of the parent scale.

For example, we have the notes of the C major scale (C D E F G A B C/1 2 3 4 5 6 7); and we choose to play them by using D as the root. This leaves us with the same exact notes as the C major scale except that our new root is D (D E F G A B C D). Once these notes are analyzed in relation to the new root we are left with the intervallic formula 1 2 b3 4 5 6 b7. This series of notes are referred to as the Dorian scale or mode. To figure out the modes from each of the seven scale degrees that stem from the major scale we must follow the exact same steps.

Even though the notes are essentially the same, the sound is completely different. Some modes seem happier/brighter while others seem darker/moodier and others bring forth a sense of dreaminess.

With the major scale, the most commonly used modes are Ionian (the major scale) and Aeolian (the natural minor scale). Other modes like Dorian, Phrygian, Lydian and Mixolydian are also quite common in certain genres. Locrian on the other hand can be a bit harder to find in most music circles.

Below I've provided a reference table with the name, intervallic formula, whole tone/half tone formula and root chord of each mode contained within the major scale.

Scale Name	Intervallic Formula	W/H Formula	Root Chord
Ionian (major scale)	1 2 3 4 5 6 7	W W H W W W H	Maj7
Dorian	1 2 b3 4 5 6 b7	W H W W W H W	Min7
Phrygian	1 b2 b3 4 5 b6 b7	H W W W H W W	Min7
Lydian	1 2 3 #4 5 6 7	W W W H W W H	Maj7
Mixolydian	1 2 3 4 5 6 b7	W W H W W H W	Dom7
Aeolian (minor scale)	1 2 b3 4 5 b6 b7	W H W W H W W	Min7
Locrian	1 b2 b3 4 b5 b6 b7	H W W H W W W	Min7(b5)

It is important to have a good grasp of the scale name, intervallic formula and root chord of each of these modes so that you may fully understand the application of the concepts to come. The whole tone/half tone formula is not such an essential category as the others within the table (in a practical purpose), but it does not hurt to have an understanding of this as well.

1. Major Scale Packs (triad/pentatonic/heptatonic)

This section of the book, which I've titled Major Scale Packs, is nothing more than a set of different pieces of information that I have found to be essential in having a real understanding of any scale. I came across the unification of this information as "packs" while teaching.

A lot of students seem to see arpeggios, triads, pentatonic scales and heptatonic scales as completely unrelated. This becomes a problem once it's time to apply such material in a practical manner. It is for this reason that I have tried to display this information in a clearer way; demonstrating the three concepts of triads, pentatonics and seven note scales one after the other in an overlapping fashion.

Before we get into the actual patterns, I'll explain why this overlapping relationship occurs within the three concepts.

Triad

A triad is nothing more than a chord constructed of three notes. These notes are chosen by stacking thirds one over the other on a certain root. The resulting triad is composed of the root, the 3rd and the 5th scale degrees of the chosen root (1 3 5). The resulting triad will vary depending on the type of 3rd or 5th within the chord. The most common triads are major (1 3 5), minor (1 b3 5), augmented (1 3 #5) and diminished (1 b3 b5).

Major	Minor	Augmented	Diminished
1 3 5	1 b3 5	1 3 #5	1 b3 b5

Pentatonic Scale

Technically a pentatonic scale is a scale composed of five notes. In the traditional fashion, the major pentatonic scale has a construction of 1 2 3 5 6; while the minor pentatonic scale has a construction of 1 b3 4 5 b7.

Major Pentatonic Scale	Minor Pentatonic Scale
1 2 3 5 6	1 b3 4 5 b7

The way I want you to visualize pentatonic scales (at least for understanding purposes) is as a triad with two added notes.

- triad + 2 added notes = pentatonic scale

In the case of the major pentatonic scale we use the major triad (1 3 5) as a base and add the 2nd and 6th degrees of the major scale to it. The ending result is 1 2 3 5 6 which is the traditional major pentatonic scale.

Triad	+ 2 added notes	= Pentatonic Scale
1 3 5	+ 2, 6	= 1 2 3 5 6

In the case of the minor pentatonic scale we begin with a minor triad (1 b3 5) as a base and add the 4th and b7th degrees of the minor scale to it. The ending result is 1 b3 4 5 b7 which is the traditional minor pentatonic scale.

Triad	2 added notes	Pentatonic Scale
1 b3 5	+ 4, b7	= 1 b3 4 5 b7

Now the major scale and its modes use mostly the major and minor pentatonic scales as their base. But there is one specific mode which acts a bit differently. Since Locrian has a b5th in it, it can't really have a minor or major pentatonic scale within it. So in this case we'll be using a modified pentatonic scale called the Min7(b5) pentatonic scale. This scale uses the minor pentatonic scale as a base and modifies its 5th degree by adding a flat to it; resulting in a b5th. The resulting intervallic construction is 1 b3 4 b5 b7.

Triad	2 added notes	Min7(b5) Pentatonic Scale
1 b3 b5	+ 4, b7	= 1 b3 4 b5 b7

Heptatonic Scale

Finally, we have the traditional heptatonic scale which is nothing more than a scale composed of seven notes. Here we have the major, melodic minor, harmonic minor and harmonic major scales and their respective modes.

As with the pentatonic scale, I want to present a new perspective on the traditional heptatonic scale. I want you to think of these scales as pentatonic scales with an added two notes.

- pentatonic scale + two added notes = heptatonic scale

In the case of the major scale we use a major pentatonic scale (1 2 3 5 6) as a base, and then we add the final 4th and 7th degrees to top off the major scale at 1 2 3 4 5 6 7.

Pentatonic Scale	2 added notes	Major Scale
1 2 3 5 6	+ 4, 7	= 1 2 3 4 5 6 7

In the case of the minor scale we use the minor pentatonic scale (1 b3 4 5 b7) as a base and add in the final 2nd and b6th degrees to complete the natural minor scale at 1 2 b3 4 5 b6 b7.

Pentatonic Scale	2 added notes	Minor Scale
1 b3 4 5 b7	+ 2, b6	= 1 2 b3 4 5 b6 b7

As mentioned in the prerequisites section of the book, this whole book uses the assistance of the CAGED system to thoroughly cover the guitar neck as a whole. This means that all of the scales and modes depicted below go through a series of five patterns of octaves that when put together, like a puzzle, end up covering the whole fretboard.

The process of connecting the triad, pentatonic scale and heptatonic scale goes through all five patterns of the CAGED system and all seven modes of the major scale.

Triad > Pentatonic Scale > Heptatonic Scale

This table displays the major scale and its modes going from triad, to pentatonic scale, to full heptatonic scale.

Triad	Pentatonic Scale	Heptatonic Scale
Major 1 3 5	Major 1 2 3 5 6	Ionian (major scale) 1 2 3 4 5 6 7
Minor 1 b3 5	Minor 1 b3 4 5 b7	Dorian 1 2 b3 4 5 6 b7
Minor 1 b3 5	Minor 1 b3 4 5 b7	Phrygian 1 b2 b3 4 5 b6 b7
Major 1 3 5	Major 1 2 3 5 6	Lydian 1 2 3 #4 5 6 7
Major 1 3 5	Major 1 2 3 5 6	Mixolydian 1 2 3 4 5 6 b7
Minor 1 b3 5	Minor 1 b3 4 5 b7	Aeolian (minor scale) 1 2 b3 4 5 b6 b7
Diminished 1 b3 b5	Min7(b5) 1 b3 4 b5 b7	Locrian 1 b2 b3 4 b5 b6 b7

Scale Diagrams

Ionian (major) Scale Pack:

Major Triad	Major Pentatonic	Ionian (major scale)
1 3 5	1 2 3 5 6	1 2 3 4 5 6 7

Pattern 1

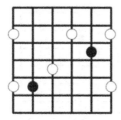 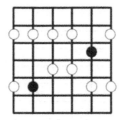 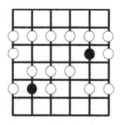

Pattern 2

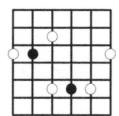 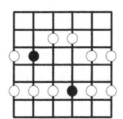 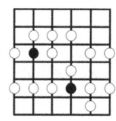

Pattern 3

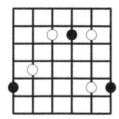 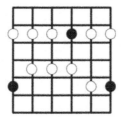 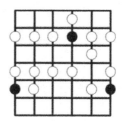

Pattern 4

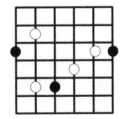 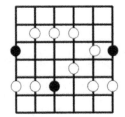 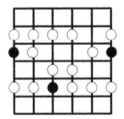

Pattern 5

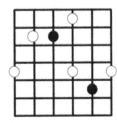 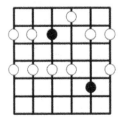 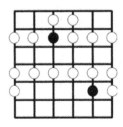

Exercise

C Ionian (major scale)

Dorian Scale Pack:

Minor Triad	Minor Pentatonic	Dorian
1 b3 5	1 b3 4 5 b7	1 2 b3 4 5 6 b7

Pattern 1

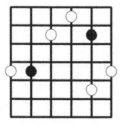 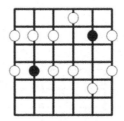 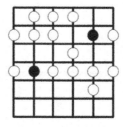

Pattern 2

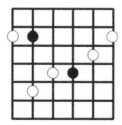 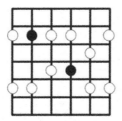 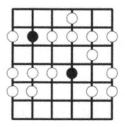

Pattern 3

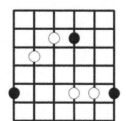 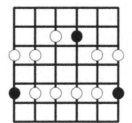 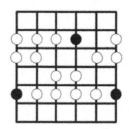

Pattern 4

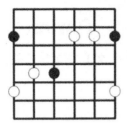 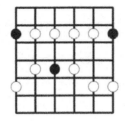 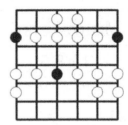

Pattern 5

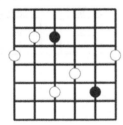 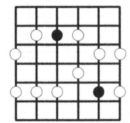 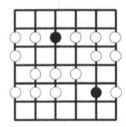

Exercise

G Dorian

Phrygian Scale Pack:

Minor Triad	Minor Pentatonic	Phrygian
1 b3 5	1 b3 4 5 b7	1 b2 b3 4 5 b6 b7

Pattern 1

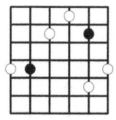 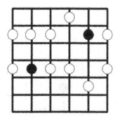 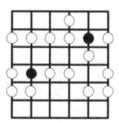

Pattern 2

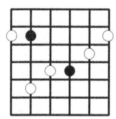 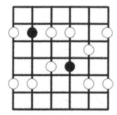 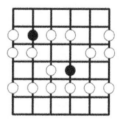

Pattern 3

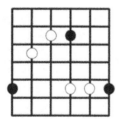 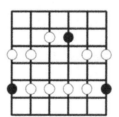 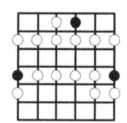

Pattern 4

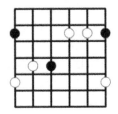 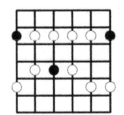 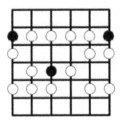

Pattern 5

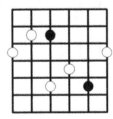 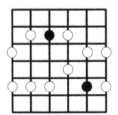 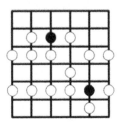

Exercise

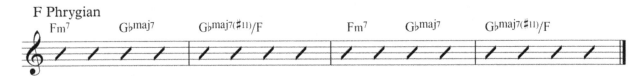

Lydian Scale Pack:

Major Triad	Major Pentatonic	Lydian
1 3 5	1 2 3 5 6	1 2 3 #4 5 6 7

Pattern 1

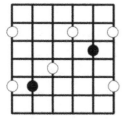 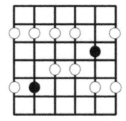 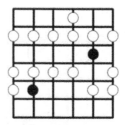

Pattern 2

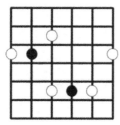 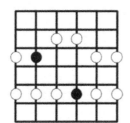 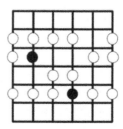

Pattern 3

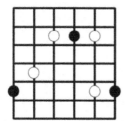 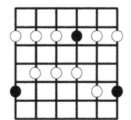 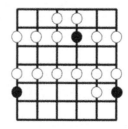

Pattern 4

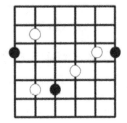 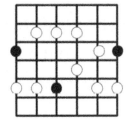 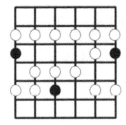

Pattern 5

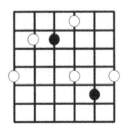 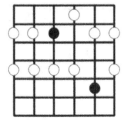 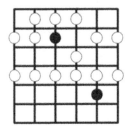

Exercise

Ab Lydian

Mixolydian Scale Pack:

Major Triad	Major Pentatonic	Mixolydian
1 3 5	1 2 3 5 6	1 2 3 4 5 6 b7

Pattern 1

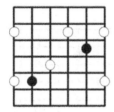 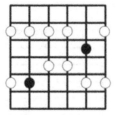 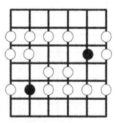

Pattern 2

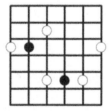 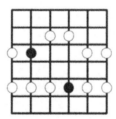 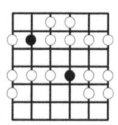

Pattern 3

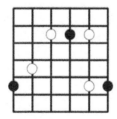 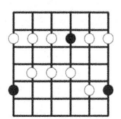 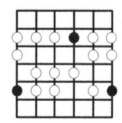

Pattern 4

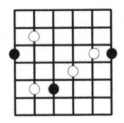 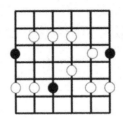 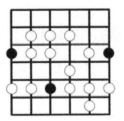

Pattern 5

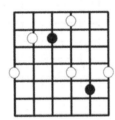 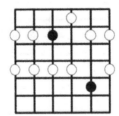 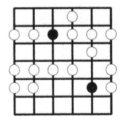

Exercise

Bb Mixolydian

Aeolian (minor) Scale Pack:

Minor Triad	Minor Pentatonic	Aeolian (minor scale)
1 b3 5	1 b3 4 5 b7	1 2 b3 4 5 b6 b7

Pattern 1

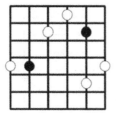 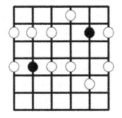 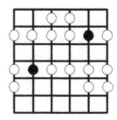

Pattern 2

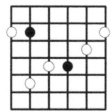 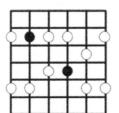 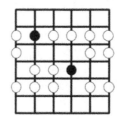

Pattern 3

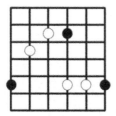 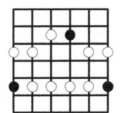 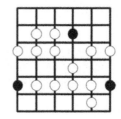

Pattern 4

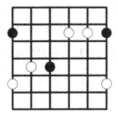 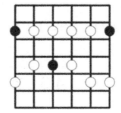 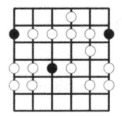

Pattern 5

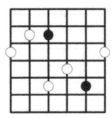 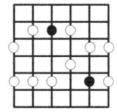 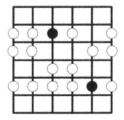

Exercise

D Aeolian (minor scale)

Locrian Scale Pack:

Diminished Triad	Min7(b5) Pentatonic	Locrian
1 b3 b5	1 b3 4 b5 b7	1 b2 b3 4 b5 b6 b7

Pattern 1

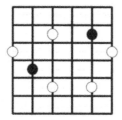 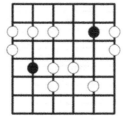 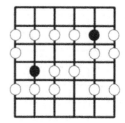

Pattern 2

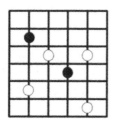 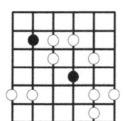 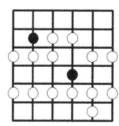

Pattern 3

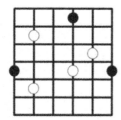 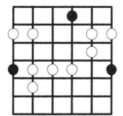 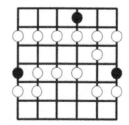

Pattern 4

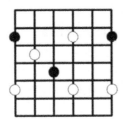 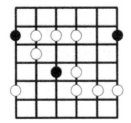 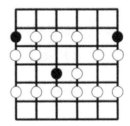

Pattern 5

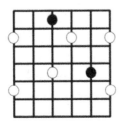 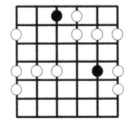 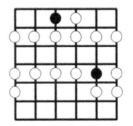

Exercise

B Locrian

Exercise and Application

- Chord progression

You can tell that right underneath each of the scale packs there is a small 4 bar chord progression. The purpose behind this chord progression is to get you started in the application of that scale or mode. My suggestion is that you either use some programming software or loop pedal to create a backing track over which you can play and practice the different concepts. This is just one chord progression to get you started; I highly suggest that you create your own and that you start applying the material over your own music.

- Learn the material

The material in this section is to be memorized, learned and fully applied. This is to be done individually with all triads, pentatonic scales and heptatonic scales; as well as with the three of them used as a whole at the same time. The whole point of this book is to create a connection between these concepts, so try to visualize all 3 concepts at the same time.

- Make the material your own

The information on this chapter is general information and is fully malleable. Learn every single diagram as written and then get to making them your own. Look for new and different ways of playing them; try different permutations, create licks, write tunes, and come up with unique phrases and combinations. This is how you'll eventually create your own style.

- Make music

Don't let the material just sit in your head stewing, make music with it. It's important to make a musical connection with every bit of new material. Really listen to what and how everything sounds like. Understand how all these different sounds make you feel and learn to use them to convey whatever feelings you want to express.

2. Harmonized Scale Weaving

It is important to first understand the concept of the harmonized scale to be able to understand the importance and reason for the "Harmonized Scale Weaving" concept. The harmonized scale is just a way of saying the diatonic chords that stem from each of the scale degrees within a scale.

These chords (7th chords in this case) are created by stacking diatonic 3rds on top of each other.

This example demonstrates the harmonized scale that results by stacking thirds in a C major scale.

The next table demonstrates the chords by using roman numerals instead of a specific key. This is done so that chord progressions and functions can be understood independently of any key. The way this works is by assigning a roman numeral to the different scale degrees of a scale and adding the specific quality (Maj7, Min7, Dom7, Min7(b5), etc.) of that chord right next to it. This results in the harmonized major scale.

Harmonized Major Scale						
Imaj7	IIm7	IIIm7	IVmaj7	V7	VIm7	VIIm7(b5)

In terms of how it's displayed on the fingerboard, I've applied what I like to call "Scale Weaving". I like the name weaving because it implies two different threads that come together to form something new (piece of cloth/basket/etc.). In this case the threads are the major scale and the harmonized major scale (through 7th arpeggios). The end result of this weaving is a further understanding of the close relationship between scales, chord tones and arpeggios.

The way that these are displayed is by portraying the specific scale, mode or octave (depending on the specific concept) in a diagram at the top of the page; while displaying the arpeggios for all of the seven scale degrees within that scale. The notes within the arpeggio are presented in grey dots, the scale in white dots and the root of the arpeggio is in black.

◯ 7th Arpeggio

◯ Scale or mode

● Root of the 7th arpeggio

Vertical Harmonized Scale

Since there are many ways to visualize the fretboard, the diagrams have been split in two sections; the vertical harmonized scale and the horizontal harmonized scale. The first of the two is the vertical harmonized scale.

The way the vertical harmonized scale is displayed is by utilizing all 5 patterns of the CAGED system and laying out the seven arpeggios that stem from each scale degree of the major scale. For example, take the CAGED system's pattern 1 of the major scale. That pattern is portrayed at the top of the page and below it appears the same pattern of the scale, but on each of the seven diagrams there is a different arpeggio that is built from a different scale degree.

Remember to practice this is in all of the keys of the major scale.

Scale Diagrams

Vertical Harmonized Major Scale (Pattern 1)

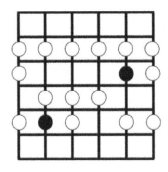

Imaj7   IIm7   IIIm7   IVmaj7

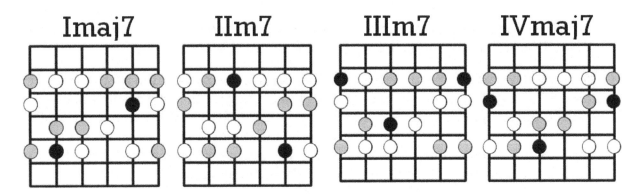

V7   VIm7   VIIm7(b5)

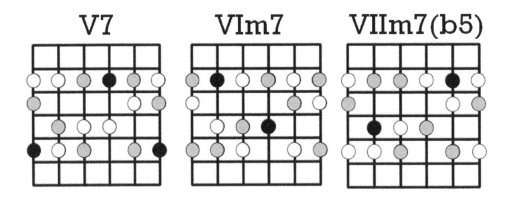

Vertical Harmonized Major Scale (Pattern 2)

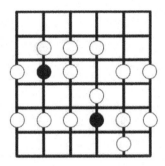

Imaj7   IIm7   IIIm7   IVmaj7

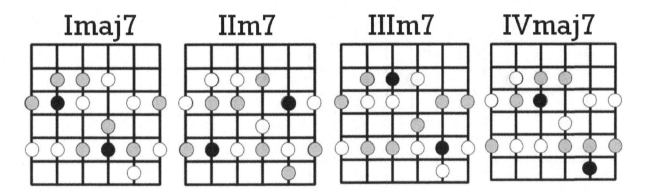

V7   VIm7   VIIm7(b5)

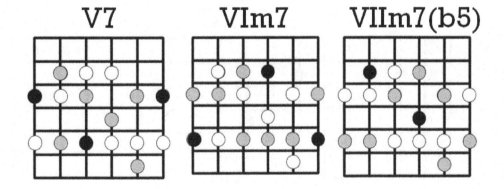

Vertical Harmonized Major Scale (Pattern 3)

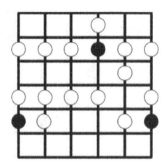

Imaj7   IIm7   IIIm7   IVmaj7

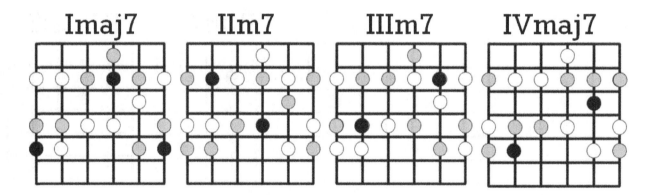

V7   VIm7   VIIm7(b5)

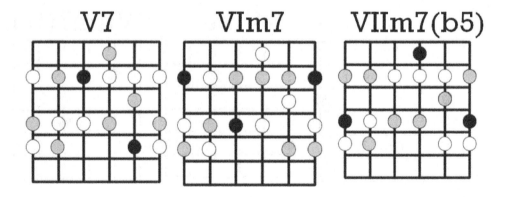

Vertical Harmonized Major Scale (Pattern 4)

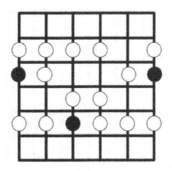

Imaj7   IIm7   IIIm7   IVmaj7

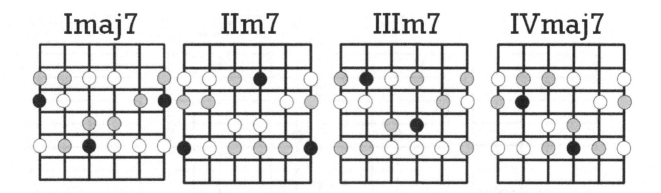

V7   VIm7   VIIm7(b5)

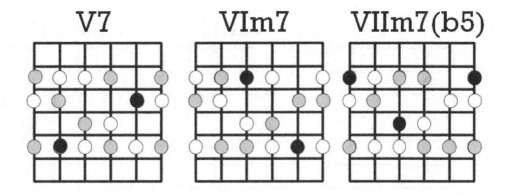

Vertical Harmonized Major Scale (Pattern 5)

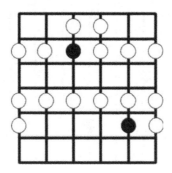

Imaj7   IIm7   IIIm7   IVmaj7

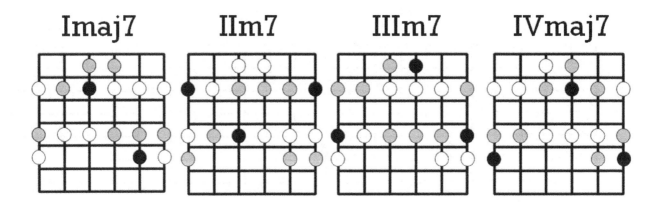

V7   VIm7   VIIm7(b5)

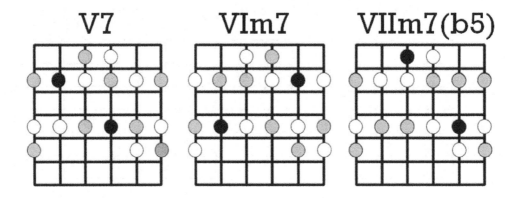

Exercise and Application

- Learn the harmonized scale order

Learn all five CAGED scale patterns with their seven respective arpeggios in their order. So play the Imaj7 arpeggio, followed by the IIm7, then the IIIm7 and so on until you reach the octave. You can use a metronome once familiarized with the patterns to create fluidity and cleanness.

- Practice shifting between specific arpeggios and the scale

You can practice each arpeggio on their own and how they feel as you shift between the scale and that one specific arpeggio. This is to be repeated on all five positions of the CAGED pattern and all seven of the arpeggios of the scale.

Also practice shifting between the seven arpeggios and the notes of the scale.

- Practice over Jazz Standards and other tunes

Apply the arpeggios and scale over your favorite jazz standards and/or any other tune to add a more practical approach of the material. Follow the chords of the tunes with just the arpeggios over one of the CAGED scale patterns. You can also practice flowing/shifting between the arpeggios and scales over the same tunes.

You can also practice this over common chord progressions like the blues and major and minor II V I's

This is to be repeated over all five patterns of the CAGED scale patterns.

- Write your own tunes

Get creative with the material; don't be shy about writing your own tunes with the use of the vertical harmonized scale.

Horizontal Harmonized Scale

The way the horizontal harmonized scale is pictured is by displaying one of the five specific octave shapes of the CAGED system and showing below it the seven arpeggios that stem from the major scale on that specific octave. In this case the major scale has to be visualized as running through the same string.

For example, take the notes in C major. Let's work on playing that scale up the 5th string. It would look something like this.

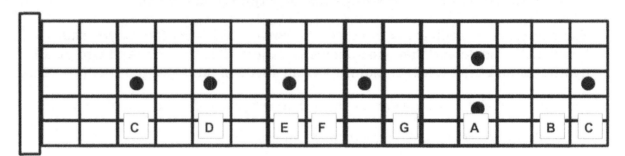

Once having visualized the scale over one string in a horizontal fashion, the next step is to visualize and practice the positioning of both the major scale and the seven arpeggios that stem from that scale.

Another way to look at it (in this case) is by starting from the C in the 3rd fret and playing both the arpeggio of the Imaj7 chord (using the pattern 1 octave of the CAGED system) and the major scale pattern over which that arpeggio appears. Next go to the D note in the 5th and play both the arpeggio of the IIm7 chord (using the pattern 1 octave of the CAGED system) and the major scale pattern over which that arpeggio appears. Then keep repeating this process until you complete the scale by reaching the C note at the 15th fret.

This process is to be repeated on all five octaves of the CAGED system, all six strings of the instrument and all twelve keys of the major scale.

Horizontal Harmonized Major Scale (Pattern 1)

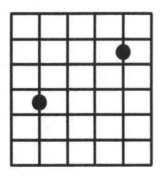

Imaj7   IIm7   IIIm7   IVmaj7

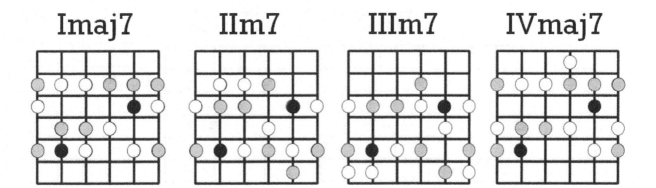

V7   VIm7   VIIm7(b5)

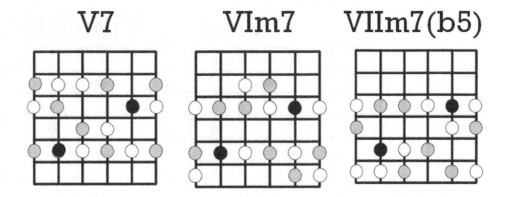

Horizontal Harmonized Major Scale (Pattern 2)

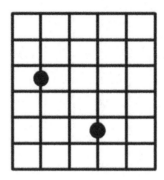

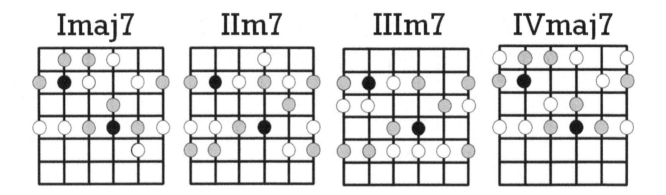

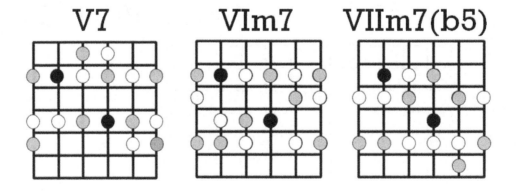

Horizontal Harmonized Major Scale (Pattern 3)

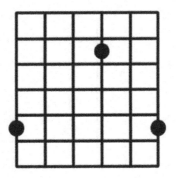

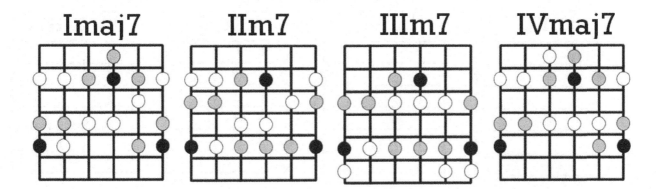

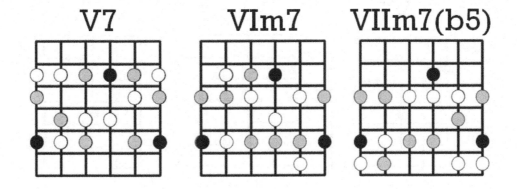

Horizontal Harmonized Major Scale (Pattern 4)

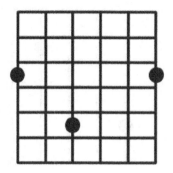

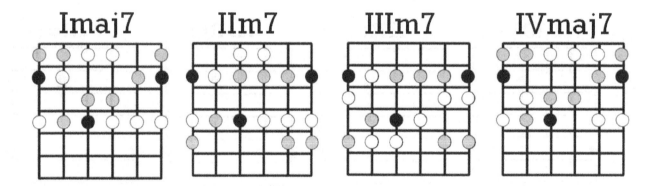

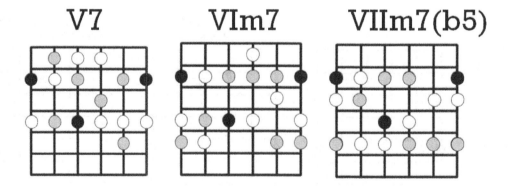

Horizontal Harmonized Major Scale (Pattern 5)

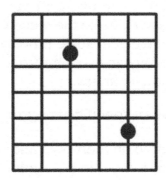

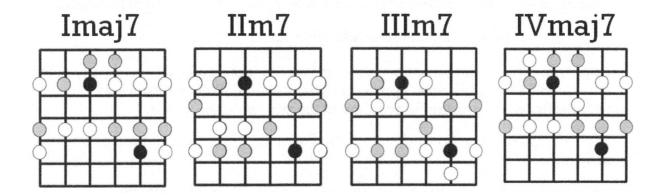

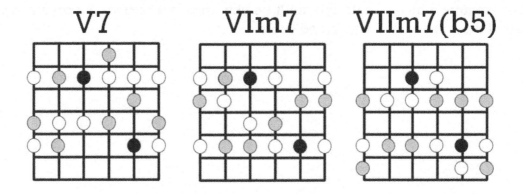

Exercise and Application

- Learn the harmonized scale order

Learn all seven arpeggios in order over the same string root. Play the Imaj7 arpeggio, followed by the IIm7, then the IIIm7 and so on until you reach the octave. This time you will be sticking to the same CAGED octave for the arpeggios. This means that the actual scale patterns will be shifting just on just about every new arpeggio. You can use a metronome once familiarized with the patterns to create fluidity and cleanness.

- Practice shifting between specific arpeggios and the scale

You can practice each arpeggio on their own and how they feel as you shift between the scale and that one specific arpeggio. This is to be repeated on all seven of the arpeggios of the scale and all five octaves of the CAGED system.

Also practice shifting between the seven arpeggios and the notes of the scale.

- Practice over Jazz Standards and other tunes

Apply the arpeggios and scale over your favorite jazz standards and/or any other tune to add a more practical approach of the material. Follow the chords of the tunes with just the arpeggios over one of the strings on the guitar.

You can also practice flowing/shifting between the arpeggios and scales over the same tunes.

This is to be repeated over all 5 patterns of the CAGED scale patterns.

- Write your own tunes

Get creative with the material; don't be shy about writing your own tunes with the use of the horizontal harmonized scale.

3. Pentatonic Scale Weaving

As mentioned in the "Major Packs" section of the book, there is a tight relationship between the Pentatonic and Heptatonic scales. Being that most guitarists lean on the pentatonic scale as a base, I decided to create a system of "weaving" in between both of the scales. Maintaining a certain pentatonic perspective as a base and peppering in some added notes from different scales and their modes.

This resulted in what I like to call "Pentatonic Scale Weaving", a system of scale diagrams that clearly depict the notes of the pentatonic scale that resides within the normal heptatonic scales that we already know. This works through a system of color coded dots where the notes of the pentatonic scale are depicted in one color (grey) while the rest of the heptatonic scale is depicted in another (white). The root of both of these scales is depicted as black.

⬤ Pentatonic scale

◯ Scale or mode

⬤ Root of the scale

Pentatonic Scale > Heptatonic Scale

Modal Order	Pentatonic Scale	Heptatonic Scale
1	Major 1 2 3 5 6	Ionian (major scale) 1 2 3 4 5 6 7
2	Minor 1 b3 4 5 b7	Dorian 1 2 b3 4 5 6 b7
3	Minor 1 b3 4 5 b7	Phrygian 1 b2 b3 4 5 b6 b7
4	Major 1 2 3 5 6	Lydian 1 2 3 #4 5 6 7
5	Major 1 2 3 5 6	Mixolydian 1 2 3 4 5 6 b7
6	Minor 1 b3 4 5 b7	Aeolian (minor scale) 1 2 b3 4 5 b6 b7
7	Min7(b5) 1 b3 4 b5 b7	Locrian 1 b2 b3 4 b5 b6 b7

Scale Diagrams

Ionian (major scale) w/ Major Pentatonic Weaving

Major Pentatonic	Ionian (major scale)
1 2 3 5 6	1 2 3 4 5 6 7

- **Chords to play over: Major, Maj7, Maj13, etc.**

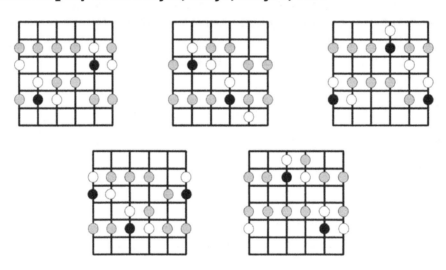

Exercise

G Ionian (major scale)

Dorian w/ Minor Pentatonic Weaving

Minor Pentatonic	Dorian
1 b3 4 5 b7	1 2 b3 4 5 6 b7

- **Chords to play over: Minor, Min7, Min11, Min13, etc.**

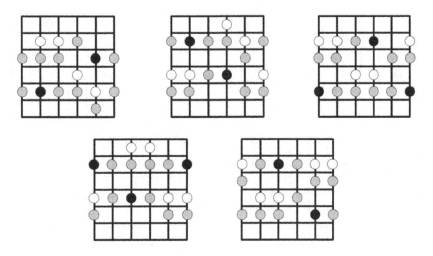

Exercise

D Dorian

Phrygian w/ Minor Pentatonic Weaving

Minor Pentatonic	Phrygian
1 b3 4 5 b7	1 b2 b3 4 5 b6 b7

- **Chords to play over: Minor, Min7, Sus4(b9), etc.**

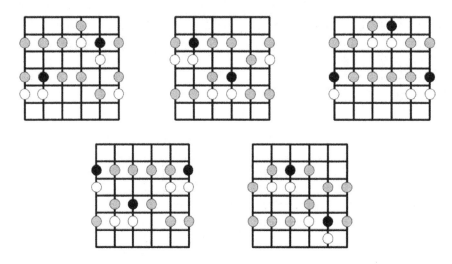

Exercise

C Phrygian

Lydian w/ Major Pentatonic Weaving

Major Pentatonic	Lydian
1 2 3 5 6	1 2 3 #4 5 6 7

- **Chords to play over: Major, Maj7, Maj7(#11), Maj9(#11), Maj13(#11), etc.**

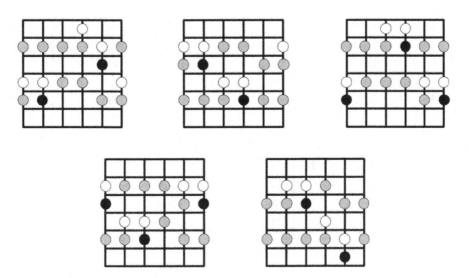

Exercise

Db Lydian

Mixolydian w/ Major Pentatonic Weaving

Major Pentatonic	Mixolydian
1 2 3 5 6	1 2 3 4 5 6 b7

- **Chords to play over: Major, Dom7, Dom9, Dom11, Dom13, Dom7(sus4), etc.**

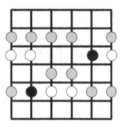 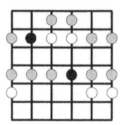 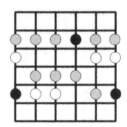

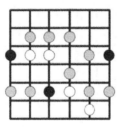 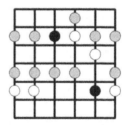

Exercise

F# Mixolydian

Aeolian (minor scale) w/ Minor Pentatonic Weaving

Minor Pentatonic	Aeolian (minor scale)
1 b3 4 5 b7	1 2 b3 4 5 b6 b7

- **Chords to play over: Minor, Min7, Min7(b13), Min7(#5), Min9, Min11, etc.**

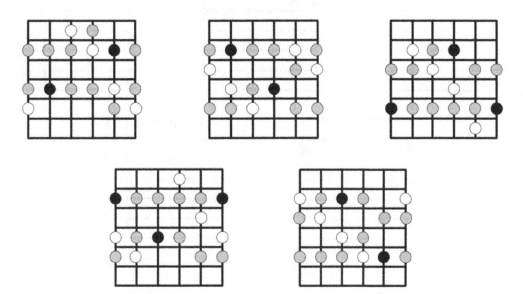

Exercise

E Aeolian (minor scale)

Locrian w/ Min7(b5) Pentatonic Weaving

Min7(b5) Pentatonic	Locrian
1 b3 4 b5 b7	1 b2 b3 4 b5 b6 b7

- **Chords to play over: Diminished triad, Min7(b5), Min7(b9, b5), etc.**

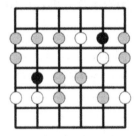
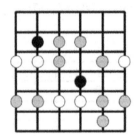
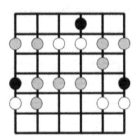

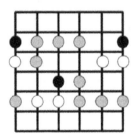
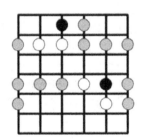

Exercise

C# Locrian

Exercise and Application

- Chord progression

The chord progression at the end of each piece of material is just one of many others that you can create yourself. Remember to practice the material over as many keys as possible. It's also important to look at as many possibilities as you can find and exploit the ones that you prefer. Practice the material individually and as a whole.

The backing chord progression makes things a bit more musical and a bit less technical so that you can have a bit more fun.

- Learn the material to its fullest

This section of the book is meant to create a bond between your pentatonic scale vocabulary and your more linear scale vocabulary. Really study the way that both heptatonic and pentatonic scales relate to each other. Which notes coincide between both scales? Which notes are different? Make sure that you understand each of what goes where, and why.

- Make music

Create some music using the new tools that you now have at your disposal. Add new colors and sounds to your already established pentatonic vocabulary. Experiment with the way these new notes change the sound properties of the pentatonic scale and write some tunes based around that sound.

4. Pentatonic Substitutions for Major Modes

Introduction

I was introduced into the topic of pentatonic substitutions by one of my guitar professors at college; Alex Machacek. The main idea behind this specific substitution concept is that three completely different major or minor pentatonic scales can be played over one chord.

The theory behind it is simple; the notes within those three pentatonic scales make up the notes within the certain mode behind that chord.

For example, let's take a Maj7 chord; this Maj7 chord is functioning as an Ionian chord and it is common knowledge than you can play a major pentatonic scale starting from the root of that chord as a means of improvisation. What's not as commonly known is that there are two other major pentatonic scales than can be played over that same chord. These other two scales though, are rooted from other degrees within the scale. In the case of Ionian, the other scale degrees are the 4th and the 5th. So in total you have three different major pentatonic scales that you can play over a Maj7chord that functions as an Ionian chord; one rooted from the 1st or root of the scale, one from the 4th and one from the 5th.

Why do these 3 different scales work? Let's take a Cmaj7 chord functioning as an Ionian chord as an example. The three major pentatonic scales that can be played are the ones stemming from the root (C major pentatonic), the 4th (F major pentatonic) and the 5th (G major pentatonic). Now, let's take a look at the notes within the Ionian scale as well as the notes within these three pentatonic scales and compare them.

C Ionian: C D E F G A B = 1 2 3 4 5 6 7

C major pentatonic: C D E G A = 1 2 3 5 6

F major pentatonic: F G A C D = 4 5 6 1 2

G major pentatonic: G A B D E = 5 6 7 2 3

After taking a look at all four scales we can tell that all the notes within these three pentatonic scales are contained within the Ionian scale. Not only that, but if we combine the notes within the three scales, the end result is the Ionian scale. The same concept is then applied accordingly to each of the modes of the major scale.

The pentatonic scales will vary from major or minor depending on the mode that is in play. In the case of the Ionian mode (major scale), the scale that is applied is the major pentatonic scale since it is a major mode. But in the case of a minor mode such as Aeolian and/or Dorian the pentatonic scale in play will be the minor pentatonic scale. This is done to maintain a clear look into the close relationship between these three pentatonic and the parent mode or scale.

Application/Diagram explanation

Now that the theory behind the concept is clear, we can take on the tables and diagrams that follow. To make things as clear as possi ble I decided to apply the scale weaving concept explained in the Pentatonic Weaving concept. The way the patterns work is by utilizing grey dots as the pentatonic scale within the diagram, white dots for the rest of the scale/mode, grey dots with a blackened rim as the root of the pentatonic substitute and black dots as the root of the scale or mode (and pentatonic scales that have the same root as the scale).

Pentatonic scale

Scale or mode

Pentatonic substitution root

Root of the scale

Scale Diagrams

Ionian

The three pentatonic scales that fit within the Ionian scale are the ones mentioned previously in the introduction of this section of the book. But to make a quick recap; since this is a major mode the scale that will be in use is the major pentatonic scale. The three pentatonic scales within the Ionian mode (major scale) are the one beginning from the root of the scale, one beginning from the 4th of the scale and finally one beginning at the 5th of the scale.

Ionian from the root

The first of the pentatonic scales is the one stemming from the root of the scale. The relationship between the parent scale and this pentatonic scale works as 1 2 3 5 6.

Major Pentatonic from the root	Ionian (major scale)
1 2 3 5 6	1 2 3 4 5 6 7

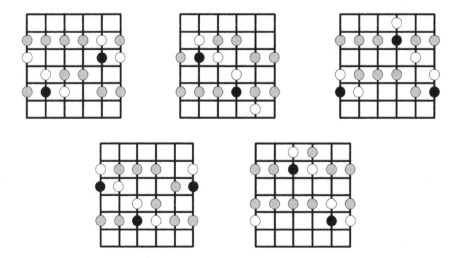

Exercise

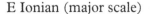
E Ionian (major scale)

Ionian from the 4th

The second of the Ionian pentatonic scales stems from the 4th degree of the scale. The intervallic relationship between the major pentatonic scale that stems from the 4th is 4 5 6 1 2 (when kept in the order of the root of the pentatonic scale)

*Caution with the use of the 4th degree in this scale as it's an avoid note and as the name implies, it should be avoided.

Major Pentatonic from the 4th	Ionian (major scale)
4 5 6 1 2	1 2 3 4 5 6 7

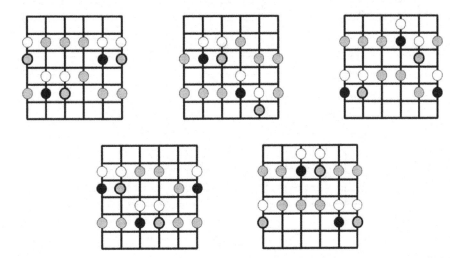

Exercise

Ab Ionian (major scale)

Ionian from the 5th

The last of the three Ionian pentatonic scales stems from the 5th degree of Ionian. The intervallic relationship of this scale and the Ionian mode works as 5 6 7 2 3 (when kept in the order of the root of the pentatonic scale).

*The root of Ionian is not part of the Pentatonic Scale

Major Pentatonic from the 5th	Ionian (major scale)
5 6 7 2 3	1 2 3 4 5 6 7

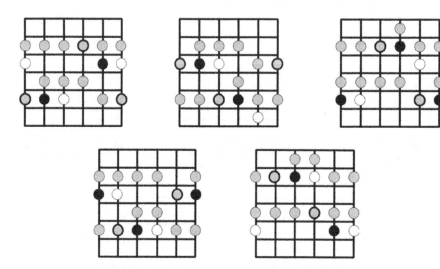

Exercise

D Ionian (major scale)

Dorian

Since the Dorian mode is considered a minor mode, the pentatonic scale that will be used is the minor pentatonic scale. The three pentatonic scales found within Dorian are the one that stems from the root, one that stems from the 2nd degree of the scale and one that stems from the 5th degree of the scale.

Dorian from the root

The first of the three Dorian pentatonic scales is the one stemming from the root. The intervallic relationship between it and Dorian works as a regular minor pentatonic scale (1 b3 4 5 b7).

Minor Pentatonic from the root	Dorian
1 b3 4 5 b7	1 2 b3 4 5 6 b7

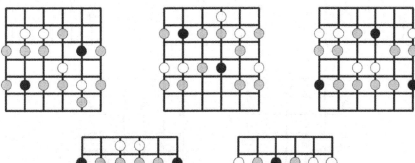

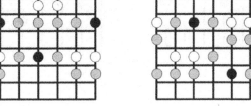

Exercise

C# Dorian

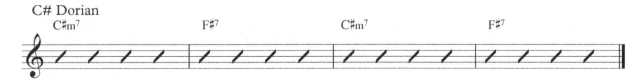

Dorian from the 2nd

The second of the Dorian pentatonic scales stems from the 2nd degree of the Dorian mode and the intervallic relationship works as 2 4 5 6 1 (when kept in the order of the root of the pentatonic scale).

*Caution with the use of the 6th degree in this scale as it's an avoid note and as the name implies, it should be avoided.

Minor Pentatonic from the 2nd	Dorian
2 4 5 6 1	1 2 b3 4 5 6 b7

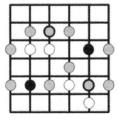
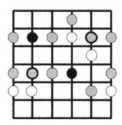
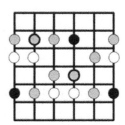

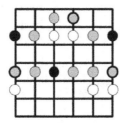
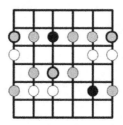

Exercise

D Dorian

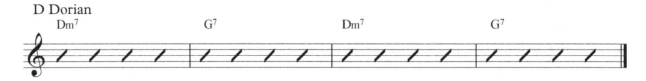

Dorian from the 5th

The final of the Dorian pentatonic scales stems from the 5th degree of the Dorian mode and the intervallic relationship works as 5 b7 1 2 4 (when kept in the order of the root of the pentatonic scale).

Minor Pentatonic from the 5th	Dorian
5 b7 1 2 4	1 2 b3 4 5 6 b7

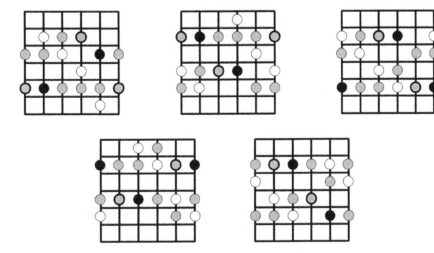

Exercise

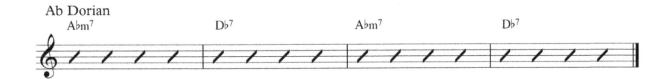

Phrygian

As with Dorian, Phrygian is a minor mode and as such the pentatonic scale to be used is the minor pentatonic scale. The three pentatonic scales which stem from Phrygian are the one from the root, one from the 4th degree of the scale and one from the b7th degree of the scale.

Phrygian from the root

The first of the Phrygian pentatonic scales is the one stemming from the root. The intervallic relationship between it and Phrygian works as a regular minor pentatonic scale (1 b3 4 5 b7).

Minor Pentatonic from the root	Phrygian
1 b3 4 5 b7	1 b2 b3 4 5 b6 b7

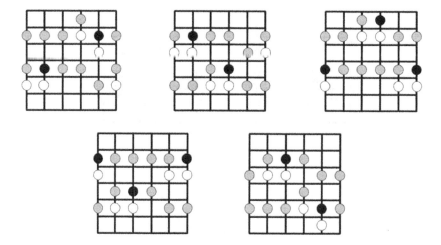

Exercise

D Phrygian

Phrygian from the 4th

The second pentatonic scale in Phrygian stems from the 4th degree of the scale and the intervallic relationship works as 4 b6 b7 1 b3 (when kept in the order of the root of the pentatonic scale).

*Caution with the use of the b6th degree in this scale as it's an avoid note and as the name implies, it should be avoided.

Minor Pentatonic from the 4th	Phrygian
4 b6 b7 1 b3	1 b2 b3 4 5 b6 b7

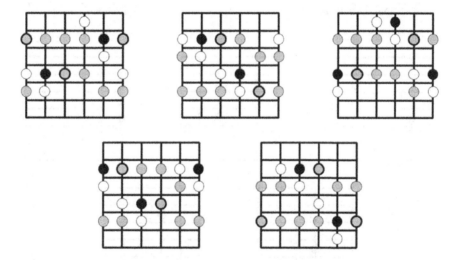

Exercise

C Phrygian

Phrygian from the b7th

The last of the Phrygian pentatonic scales is the one stemming from the b7th degree of the scale. The intervallic relationship between Phrygian and the pentatonic scale works as b7 b2 b3 4 b6 (when kept in the order of the root of the pentatonic scale).

*Caution with the use of the b2nd and b6th degrees in this scale as they're avoid notes and as the name implies, should be avoided.

*The root of Phrygian is not part of the Pentatonic Scale.

Minor Pentatonic from the b7th	Phrygian
b7 b2 b3 4 b6	1 b2 b3 4 5 b6 b7

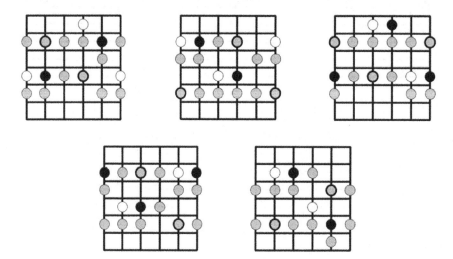

Exercise

Lydian

Lydian is a major mode and as such the pentatonic scale to be used is the major pentatonic scale. The three pentatonic scales within Lydian are the one stemming from the root, one stemming from the 2nd degree of the scale and one stemming from the 5th degree of the scale.

Lydian from the root

The first of the Lydian pentatonic scales is the one stemming from the root. The intervallic relationship between it and Lydian works the same as a regular major pentatonic scale (1 2 3 5 6).

Major Pentatonic	Lydian
1 2 3 5 6	1 2 3 #4 5 6 7

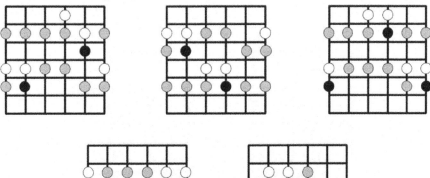

Exercise

E Lydian

Lydian from the 2nd

The second Lydian pentatonic scale is the one stemming from the 2nd degree of the scale. The intervallic relationship between it and Lydian works as 2 3 #4 6 7 (when kept in the order of the root of the pentatonic scale).

*The root of Lydian is not part of the pentatonic scale.

Major Pentatonic from the 2nd	Lydian
2 3 #4 6 7	1 2 3 #4 5 6 7

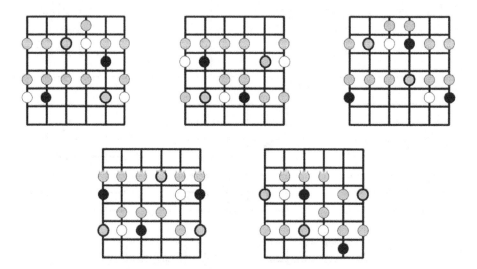

Exercise

D Lydian

Lydian from the 5ᵗʰ

The last Lydian pentatonic scale is the one stemming from the 5ᵗʰ degree of the scale. The intervallic relationship between it and Lydian works as 5 6 7 2 3 (when kept in the order of the root of the pentatonic scale).

*The root of Lydian is not part of the Pentatonic Scale.

Major Pentatonic from the 5ᵗʰ	Lydian
5 6 7 2 3	1 2 3 #4 5 6 7

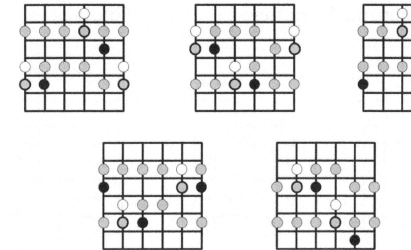

Exercise

Eb Lydian

Mixolydian

Mixolydian is a major mode and as such the pentatonic scale to be used with it is the major pentatonic scale. The three pentatonic scales within Mixolydian are the one stemming from the root, one stemming from the 4th degree of the scale and one stemming from the b7th degree of the scale.

Mixolydian from the root

The first of the Mixolydian pentatonic scales is the one from stemming from the root. The intervallic relationship works the same as a major pentatonic scale (1 2 3 5 6).

Major Pentatonic from the root	Mixolydian
1 2 3 5 6	1 2 3 4 5 6 b7

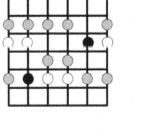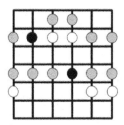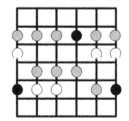

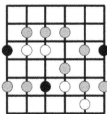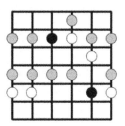

Exercise

B Mixolydian

Mixolydian from the 4th

The next pentatonic scale is the one stemming from the 4th degree of the scale. The intervallic relationship works as 4 5 6 1 2 (when kept in the order of the root of the pentatonic scale).

*Caution with the use of the 4th degree in this scale as it's an avoid note and as the name implies, it should be avoided.

Major Pentatonic from the 4th	Mixolydian
4 5 6 1 2	1 2 3 4 5 6 b7

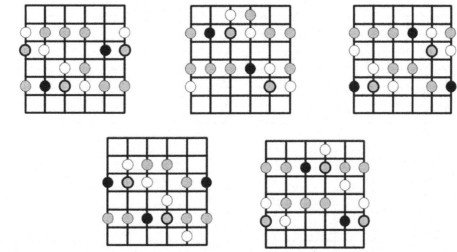

Exercise

F# Mixolydian

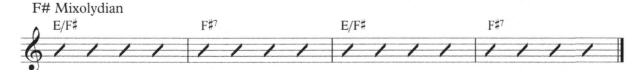

Mixolydian from the b7th

The final Mixolydian pentatonic scale is the one stemming from the b7th degree of the scale. The intervallic relationship works as b7 1 2 4 5 (when kept in the order of the root of the pentatonic scale).

*Caution with the use of the 4th degree in this scale as it's an avoid note and as the name implies, it should be avoided.

Major Pentatonic from the b7th	Mixolydian
b7 1 2 4 5	1 2 3 4 5 6 b7

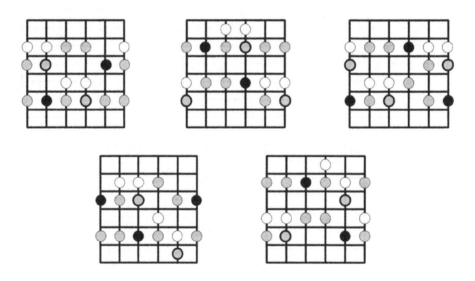

Exercise

C Mixolydian

Aeolian (natural minor scale)

Aeolian or the natural minor scale is a minor mode (as its name suggests); as such, the pentatonic scale to be used is the minor pentatonic scale. The three pentatonic scales within Aeolian are the one stemming from the root, one stemming from the 4th degree of the scale and one stemming from the 5th degree of the scale.

Aeolian from the root

The first of the Aeolian pentatonic scales is the one stemming from the root. The intervallic relationship works the same as with any minor pentatonic scale (1 b3 4 5 b7).

Minor Pentatonic from the root	Aeolian (minor scale)
1 b3 4 5 b7	1 2 b3 4 5 b6 b7

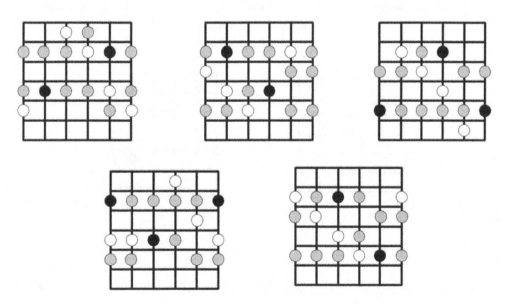

Exercise

F Aeolian (minor scale)

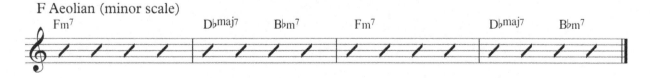

Fm⁷   D♭maj7   B♭m⁷   Fm⁷   D♭maj7   B♭m⁷

Aeolian from the 4ᵗʰ

The second Aeolian pentatonic scale is the one stemming from the 4rd degree of the scale. The intervallic relationship between it and Aeolian works as 4 b6 b7 1 b3 (when kept in the order of the root of the pentatonic scale).

*Caution with the use of the b6ᵗʰ degree in this scale as it's an avoid note and as the name implies, it should be avoided.

Minor Pentatonic from the 4ᵗʰ	Aeolian (minor scale)
4 b6 b7 1 b3	1 2 b3 4 5 b6 b7

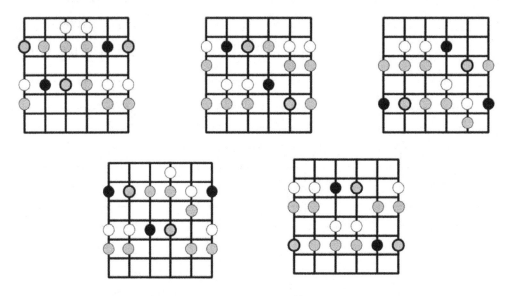

Exercise

E Aeolian (minor scale)

Aeolian from the 5ᵗʰ

The last of the Aeolian pentatonic scales is the one stemming from the 5ᵗʰ degree of the scale. The intervallic relationship between it and Aeolian works as 5 b7 1 2 4 (when kept in the order of the root of the pentatonic scale).

Minor Pentatonic from the 5ᵗʰ	Aeolian (minor scale)
5 b7 1 2 4	1 2 b3 4 5 b6 b7

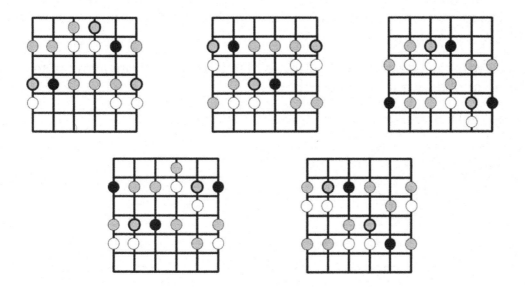

Exercise

A Aeolian (minor scale)

Locrian

Since Locrian has a b5 scale degree within it, it could be argued that it is more of a diminished mode than a minor mode. This is what makes Locrian a bit different from all the other modes of the major scale. What this means is that there will be no root pentatonic scale as with the other modes. None the less, the scale to be used over Locrian is the minor pentatonic scale. The three pentatonic scales stemming from Locrian are one from the b3rd degree of the scale, one from the 4th degree of the scale and one from the b7th degree of the scale.

Locrian from the b3rd

The first of the pentatonic scales is the one stemming from the b3rd degree of the scale. The intervallic relationship works as b3 b5 b6 b7 b2 (when kept in the order of the root of the pentatonic scale).

*Caution with the use of the b2nd degree in this scale as it's an avoid note and as the name implies, it should be avoided.

*The root of Locrian is not part of the Pentatonic Scale.

Min7(b5) Pentatonic from the b3rd	Locrian
b3 b5 b6 b7 b2	1 b2 b3 4 b5 b6 b7

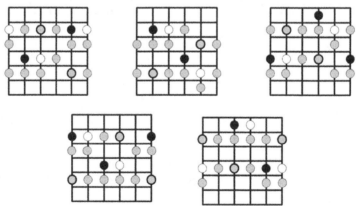

Exercise

C Locrian

Locrian from the 4th

The second of the Locrian pentatonic scales is the one stemming from the 4th degree of the scale. The intervallic relationship works as 4 b6 b7 1 b3 (when kept in the order of the root of the pentatonic scale).

Min7(b5) Pentatonic from the 4th	Locrian
4 b6 b7 1 b3	1 b2 b3 4 b5 b6 b7

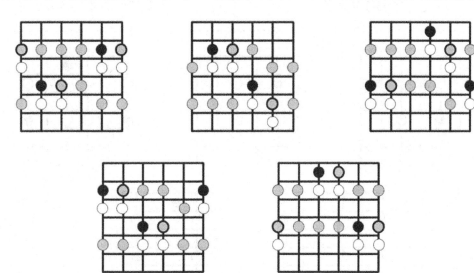

Exercise

C# Locrian

Locrian from the b7th

The last of the Locrian pentatonic scales is the one stemming from the b7th degree of the scale. The intervallic relationship works as b7 b2 b3 4 b6 (when kept in the order of the root of the pentatonic scale).

*The root of Locrian is not part of the Pentatonic Scale.

Min7(b5) Pentatonic from the b7th	Locrian
b7 b2 b3 4 b6	1 b2 b3 4 b5 b6 b7

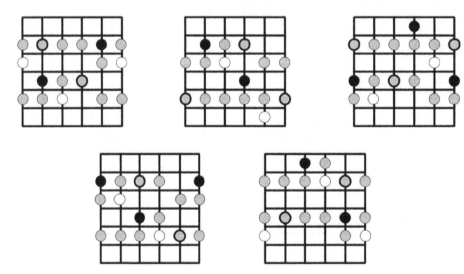

Exercise

E Locrian

Exercise and Application

- Chord Progression

The experimentation process over the chord progression and application of this section of the book is pretty important since you are dealing with a completely new application of the pentatonic scale. At times it might sound odd and you will find out that your common pentatonic scale vocabulary won't fit over each and every one of these substitutions. But that is why it's important to experiment; you want to give your ear a chance to adjust to the new sounds. Once you do that, you want to pick and choose which ones work the best for you.

It is also important to experiment with your pentatonic scale phrasing since you might find out that some of your bluesy chops won't work that well in some instances. None the less the substitutions pull through with some different style phrasing.

- Pick and choose

As mentioned in the last paragraph; this is a good way to start picking and choosing material to develop your own style. You can make sure to find some new and odd sounds since these pentatonic substitutions can be a bit uncommon at times. This makes for original and individualized sounds to base your own style from.

- Write music

I know that I mention this in just about all of the exercise and application sections of the book, but it's an absolute must! The whole point of learning new information is to apply it to your creative process. The new information is just new colors and sounds to use on your own musical canvas. You have to use them!

Chapter Two

Melodic Minor Scale and Modes

The melodic minor scale (and its modes) is definitely one of my favorite scales to access when looking to spice up my vocabulary with more jazzy/outside sounding tones. It's definitely a favored color of scale in the jazz world with some of the most used modes being Altered, Lydian Dominant and Locrian nat 2.

As with the major scale, the melodic minor scale is built up by a series of whole tones (W) and half tones (H); when put together it looks like this: W H W W W W H. But more importantly the intervallic construction of this scale is 1 2 b3 4 5 6 7.

In the classical sense this scale has two different forms; the ascending and descending. The ascending is the formula provided above (1 2 b3 4 5 6 7). The descending is the same as the natural minor scale or Aeolian mode in the major scale (1 2 b3 4 5 b6 b7). But for jazz purposes (and this books purposes), the scale remains the same both ascending and descending (1 2 b3 4 5 6 7).

As with the major scale, you can extract a set of modes from the melodic minor scale (and just about any other scale). You just have to follow the same procedure of assigning any one of the scale degrees as the root, and restarting the scale from there. Just by designating a new root within the scale you can achieve a new and different sound than that of the parent scale (in this case the melodic minor scale).

Some of the most popular modes of the melodic minor scale are Lydian Dominant, Locrian nat 2 and Altered (Altered probably being the most used of the seven). Altered is definitely one of the go to scales for going outside over a resolving Dominant 7th chord.

Here is a table with the scale name/mode name, intervallic formula, W/H formula and root chord of all the modes within the melodic minor scale.

Scale Name	Intervallic Formula	W/H Formula	Root Chord
Melodic Minor	1 2 b3 4 5 6 7	W H W W W W H	Min(maj7)
Dorian b2	1 b2 b3 4 5 6 b7	H W W W W H W	Min7
Lydian Augmented	1 2 3 #4 #5 6 7	W W W W H W H	Maj7(#5)
Lydian Dominant	1 2 3 #4 5 6 b7	W W W H W H W	Dom7
Mixolydian b6	1 2 3 4 5 b6 b7	W W H W H W W	Dom7
Locrian nat 2	1 2 b3 4 b5 b6 b7	W H W H W W W	Min7(b5)
Altered	1 b2 b3 b4 b5 b6 b7 or 1 b2 #2 3 b5 #5 b7	H W H W W W W	Min7(b5) Or Dom7(alt)

It is important to have a good grasp of the scale name, intervallic formula and root chord of each of these modes so that you may fully understand the application of the concepts to come. The whole tone/half tone formula is not such an essential category as the other categories within the table (in a practical purpose), but it does not hurt to have an understanding of this as well.

1. Melodic Minor Scale Packs (triad/pentatonic/heptatonic)

Triad

When it comes to the triads section of the melodic minor scale we find the usual suspects that were used in the major section of the book. The same major, minor, augmented and diminished triads as before.

Major	Minor	Augmented	Diminished
1 3 5	1 b3 5	1 3 #5	1 b3 b5

The only difference is that we will be working with a new type of triad that appears within the Altered mode. The new triad is a major (b5) triad which has an intervallic construction of 1 3 b5.

Major(b5)
1 3 b5

Pentatonic

The same rules applied to creating the pentatonic scales in the major scale are followed when working with the melodic minor scale. I want you to visualize the pentatonic scale as being a triad with two extra added notes.

- Minor Pentatonic

Triad	2 added notes	Pentatonic Scale
1 b3 5	+ 4, b7	= 1 b3 4 5 b7

- Major Pentatonic

Triad	+ 2 added notes	= Pentatonic Scale
1 3 5	+ 2, 6	= 1 2 3 5 6

Now while the major scale only worked with two different types of pentatonic scales that were repeated throughout the seven modes; the melodic minor scale works with a different pentatonic scale for each degree. This would result in seven different pentatonic scales. But instead of doing seven pentatonic scales I decided to do ten.

I created four different pentatonic scales that would fit within the 7th mode of the scale which is Altered. I decided to do this since there are a variety of extended chords that stem from this scale.

The new pentatonic scales and their intervallic construction are pictured in the table below.

Pentatonic Scale	Intervallic Construction	Pentatonic Scale	Intervallic Construction
Min(maj7) Pentatonic	1 b3 4 5 7	Dom7(b2, b5) Pentatonic	1 b2 3 b5 b7
Major(#5) Pentatonic	1 2 3 #5 6	Dom7(#2, #5) Pentatonic	1 #2 3 #5 b7
Major(b6) Pentatonic	1 2 3 5 b6	Dom7(b2, #5) Pentatonic	1 b2 3 #5 b7
Min7(b5) Pentatonic	1 b3 4 b5 b7	Dom7(#2, b5) Pentatonic	1 #2 3 b5 b7

The way I came across these new pentatonic scales was by modifying the original major and minor pentatonic scales to accommodate to the new scales and modes. For example, the melodic minor scale has an intervallic construction of 1 2 b3 4 5 6 7 over which neither the major (1 2 3 5 6) or minor (1 b3 4 5 b7) pentatonic scales would fit. This means that one of the two scales is to be chosen to be modified.

I decided to choose the minor pentatonic scale as a base and to modify it according to the construction of the melodic minor scale. This resulted in the removal of the flat from the b7th degree of the scale which results in a major 7th. The finished result is a pentatonic scale with an intervallic construction of 1 b3 4 5 7. The name of this scale is the Min(maj7) pentatonic scale.

It can also be viewed as selecting the triad that best fits the scale or mode and then adding in two extra note extensions that fit it. The result is also a new pentatonic scale.

Triad	2 added notes	Pentatonic Scale
1 b3 5	+ 4, 7	= 1 b3 4 5 7

This same process is done over the seven modes of the melodic minor scale.

Heptatonic

Finally, we have the full seven note melodic minor scale. As with the major scale, the perspective that I want you to have when it comes to looking at the seven note scale is that of a pentatonic scale with two added notes. In the case of the melodic minor scale we have a Min(maj7) pentatonic scale (1 b3 4 5 7) as a base and we add a major 2nd and a major 6th to complete the seven notes of the scale.

Pentatonic Scale	2 added notes	Melodic Minor Scale
1 b3 4 5 7	+ 2, 6	= 1 2 b3 4 5 6 7

This same process is then repeated with the rest of the modes of the melodic minor scale to end up with the table on the next page.

Triad > Pentatonic Scale > Heptatonic Scale

Triad	Pentatonic Scale	Heptatonic Scale
Minor 1 b3 5	Min(maj7) 1 b3 4 5 7	Melodic Minor 1 2 b3 4 5 6 7
Minor 1 b3 5	Minor 1 b3 4 5 b7	Dorian b2 1 b2 b3 4 5 6 b7
Augmented 1 3 #5	Major(#5) 1 2 3 #5 6	Lydian Augmented 1 2 3 #4 #5 6 7
Major 1 3 5	Major 1 2 3 5 6	Lydian Dominant 1 2 3 #4 5 6 b7
Major 1 3 5	Major(b6) 1 2 3 5 b6	Mixolydian b6 1 2 3 4 5 b6 b7
Diminished 1 b3 b5	Min7(b5) 1 b3 4 b5 b7	Locrian nat 2 1 2 b3 4 b5 b6 b7
Major(b5) 1 3 b5	Dom7(b2, b5) 1 b2 3 b5 b7	Altered 1 1 b2 b3 b4 b5 b6 b7 or 1 b2 #2 3 b5 #5 b7
Augmented 1 3 #5	Dom7(#2, #5) 1 #2 3 #5 b7	Altered 2 1 b2 b3 b4 b5 b6 b7 or 1 b2 #2 3 b5 #5 b7
Augmented 1 3 #5	Dom7 (b2, #5) 1 b2 3 #5 b7	Altered 3 1 b2 b3 b4 b5 b6 b7 or 1 b2 #2 3 b5 #5 b7
Major(b5) 1 3 b5	Dom7(#2, b5) 1 #2 3 b5 b7	Altered 4 1 b2 b3 b4 b5 b6 b7 or 1 b2 #2 3 b5 #5 b7

Scale Diagrams

Melodic Minor Scale Pack

Minor Triad	Min(maj7) Pentatonic	Melodic Minor
1 b3 5	1 b3 4 5 7	1 2 b3 4 5 6 7

Pattern 1

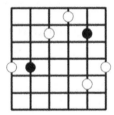 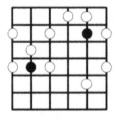 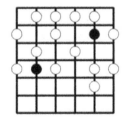

Pattern 2

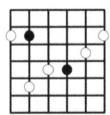 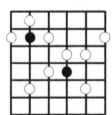 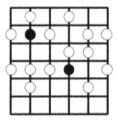

Pattern 3

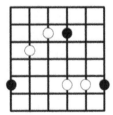 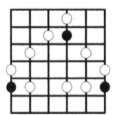 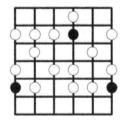

Pattern 4

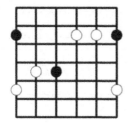
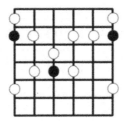
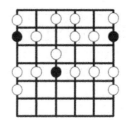

Pattern 5

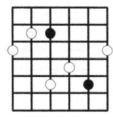
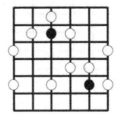
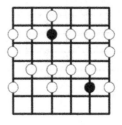

Exercise and Application

G Melodic Minor

Dorian b2 Scale Pack

Minor Triad	Minor Pentatonic	Dorian b2
1 b3 5	1 b3 4 5 b7	1 b2 b3 4 5 6 b7

Pattern 1

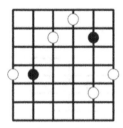 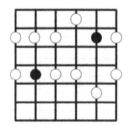 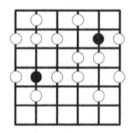

Pattern 2

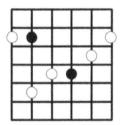 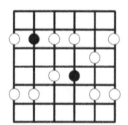 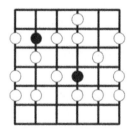

Pattern 3

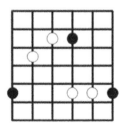 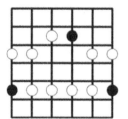 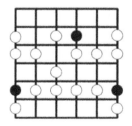

Pattern 4

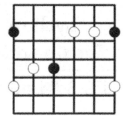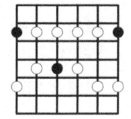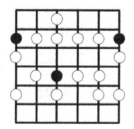

Pattern 5

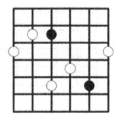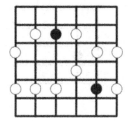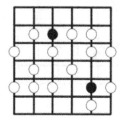

Exercise and Application

Ab Dorian b2

Lydian Augmented Scale Pack

Augmented Triad	Major (#5) Pentatonic	Lydian Augmented
1 3 #5	1 2 3 #5 6	1 2 3 #4 #5 6 7

Pattern 1

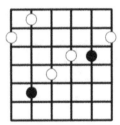 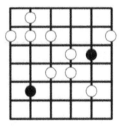 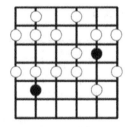

Pattern 2

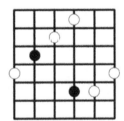 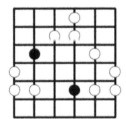 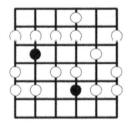

Pattern 3

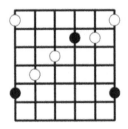 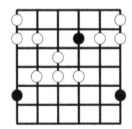 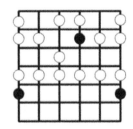

Pattern 4

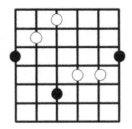 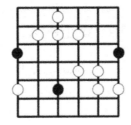 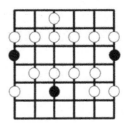

Pattern 5

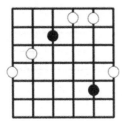 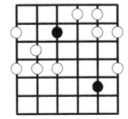 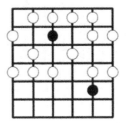

Exercise and Application

C Lydian Augmented

Lydian Dominant Scale Pack

Major Triad	Major Pentatonic	Lydian Dominant
1 3 5	1 2 3 5 6	1 2 3 #4 5 6 b7

Pattern 1

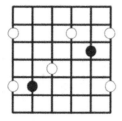 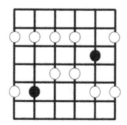 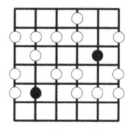

Pattern 2

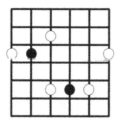 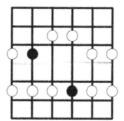 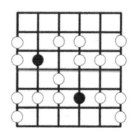

Pattern 3

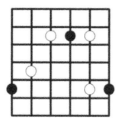 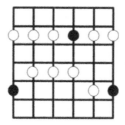 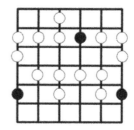

Pattern 4

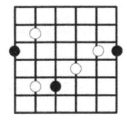 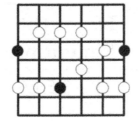 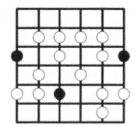

Pattern 5

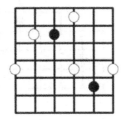 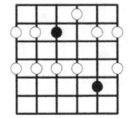 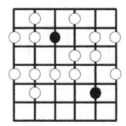

Exercise

B Lydian Dominant

Mixolydian b6 Scale Pack

Major Triad	Major (b6) Pentatonic	Mixolydian b6
1 3 5	1 2 3 5 b6	1 2 3 4 5 b6 b7

Pattern 1

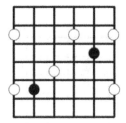 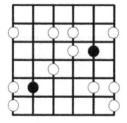 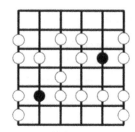

Pattern 2

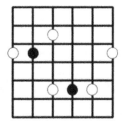 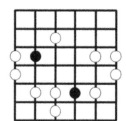 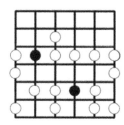

Pattern 3

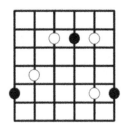 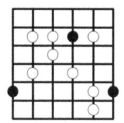 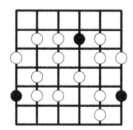

Pattern 4

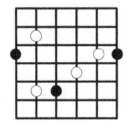 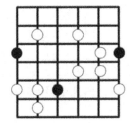 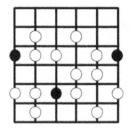

Pattern 5

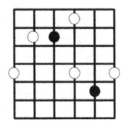 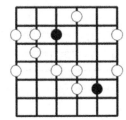 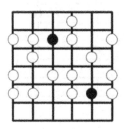

Exercise

C# Mixolydian b6

Locrian nat 2 Scale Pack

Diminished Triad	Min7(b5) Pentatonic	Locrian nat 2
1 b3 b5	1 b3 4 b5 b7	1 2 b3 4 b5 b6 b7

Pattern 1

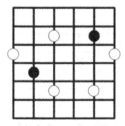 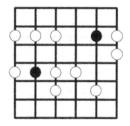 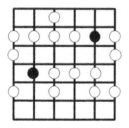

Pattern 2

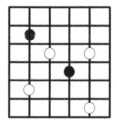 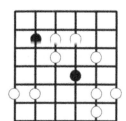 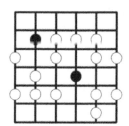

Pattern 3

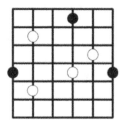 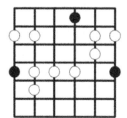 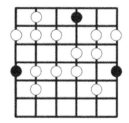

Pattern 4

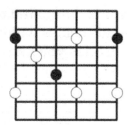 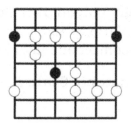 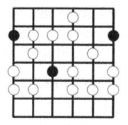

Pattern 5

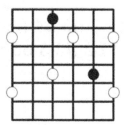 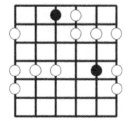 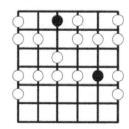

Exercise

Eb Locrian nat 2

Altered Scale Packs

Since the Altered scale is usually played over Dom7(alt) chords, I decided to include a couple of variations of triads and modified pentatonic scales within it. Play around with the different combinations to find out which ones you like best.

Altered w/Dom 7(b2, b5) Pentatonic Scale Pack

Major (b5) Triad	Dom7(b2,b5) Pentatonic	Altered
1 3 b5	1 b2 3 b5 b7	1 b2 b3 b4 b5 b6 b7 1 b2 #2 3 b5 #5 b7

Pattern 1

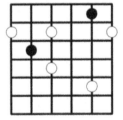 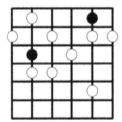 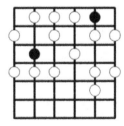

Pattern 2

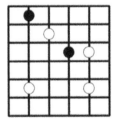 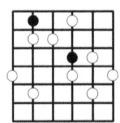 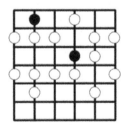

Pattern 3

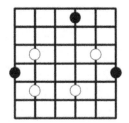 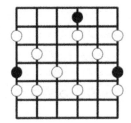 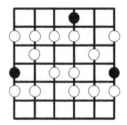

Pattern 4

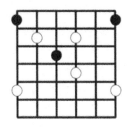 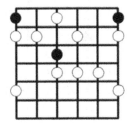 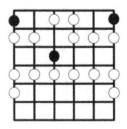

Pattern 5

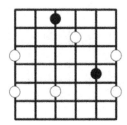 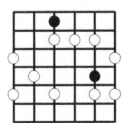 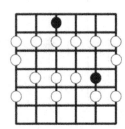

Exercise

D Altered

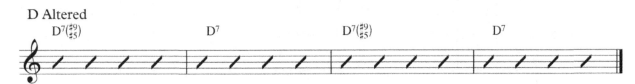

Altered w/Dom 7(#2, #5) Pentatonic Scale Pack

Augmented Triad	Dom7(#2,#5) Pentatonic	Altered
1 3 #5	1 #2 3 #5 b7	1 b2 b3 b4 b5 b6 b7 1 b2 #2 3 b5 #5 b7

Pattern 1

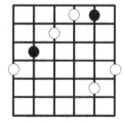 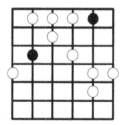 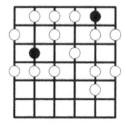

Pattern 2

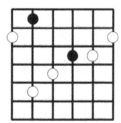 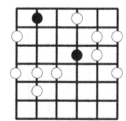 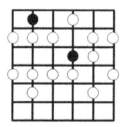

Pattern 3

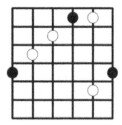 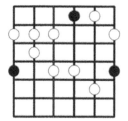 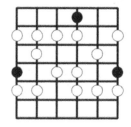

Pattern 4

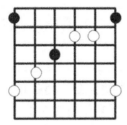 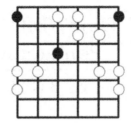 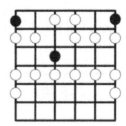

Pattern 5

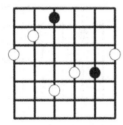 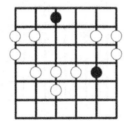 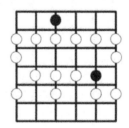

Exercise and Application

Altered w/Dom 7(b2, #5) Pentatonic Scale Pack

Augmented Triad	Dom7(b2,#5) Pentatonic	Altered
1 3 #5	1 b2 3 #5 b7	1 b2 b3 b4 b5 b6 b7 1 b2 #2 3 b5 #5 b7

Pattern 1

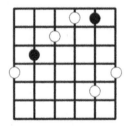 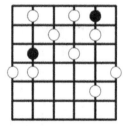 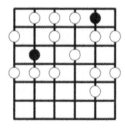

Pattern 2

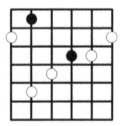 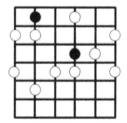 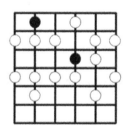

Pattern 3

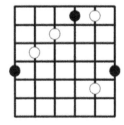 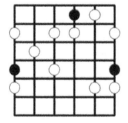 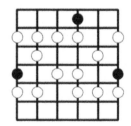

Pattern 4

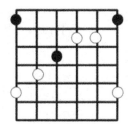 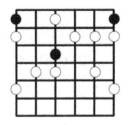 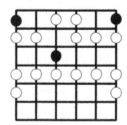

Pattern 5

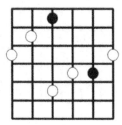 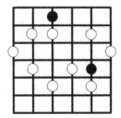 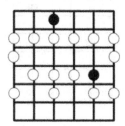

Exercise and Application

F# Altered

Altered w/Dom 7(#2, b5) Pentatonic Scale Pack

Major (b5) Triad	Dom7(#2,b5) Pentatonic	Altered
1 3 b5	1 #2 3 b5 b7	1 b2 b3 b4 b5 b6 b7 1 b2 #2 3 b5 #5 b7

Pattern 1

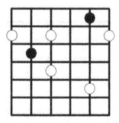 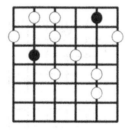 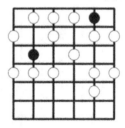

Pattern 2

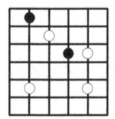 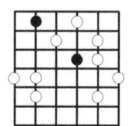 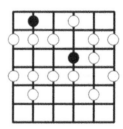

Pattern 3

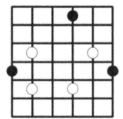 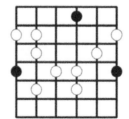 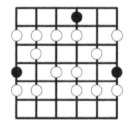

Pattern 4

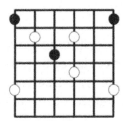
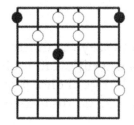
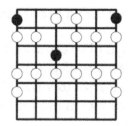

Pattern 5

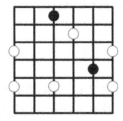
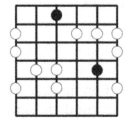
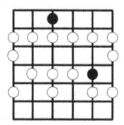

Exercise and Application

Eb Altered

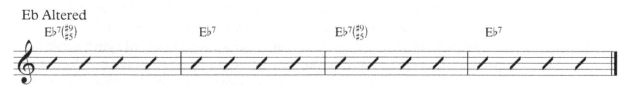

Exercise and Application

- Chord Progression

Always play around with different ways of improvisation and application over the written chord progressions. Try out different techniques, intervals, concepts and don't forget to write out some other cool chord progressions to practice over (use the chords in the following harmonized melodic minor scale section to make it easier).

- Pick and choose

As with the Pentatonic Substitutions in the major scale chapter; the melodic minor scale is a great start up scale to begin tinkering in the development of your own sound.

- Jazz (fusion) it up!

Ever wonder how a lot of jazz and fusion guys get their sound? You got it! A lot of it is the melodic minor scale and its modes. Experiment with this scale and its seven modes to find out which ones sound best for you and which ones sound a bit familiar (like some of your favorite player maybe).

It's also a great opportunity to experiment with jazz (if you haven't done so already). The use of the melodic minor scale over dominant chords with Lydian Dominant, Mixolydian b6 and Altered, as a way to spice up minor and major tonalities with Melodic Minor and Lydian Augmented and even playing over Min7(b5) chords with Locrian nat 2 make this scale an important asset when experimenting with jazz, fusion and progressive genres (don't be shy about introducing them into other genres as well).

2. Harmonized Scale Weaving

Now that we already understand the process of coming up with the harmonized scale (explained in the harmonized major scale section of the book), it's only a matter of applying the same concept to different scales. In the case of the melodic minor scale we apply the exact same process of stacking the scale in 3rds. Below is an example showing the harmonized C melodic minor scale and the different chords that result from the stacked 3rds of each of the scale degrees.

Once that is done, the resulting chords can be displayed via the use of roman numerals so that it becomes easier to transpose between different keys.

Harmonized Melodic Minor Scale						
Im(maj7)	IIm7	bIIImaj7(#5)	IV7	V7	VIm7(b5)	VIIm7(b5)

As a quick note, you might notice that over the VII chord I went with a Min7(b5) instead of a Dom7(alt) chord. Even though the Altered scale (7th mode of the melodic minor scale) is predominantly used over Dom7(alt) chords, the fact is that you get a Min7(b5) chord/arpeggio when stacking the scale in 3rds. So I decided to stay true to that construction. Never the less, keep in mind that the Min7(b5) chord could be substituted for a Dom7(alt) chord.

Once again, the book utilizes the display system of scale weaving which depicts the notes of the arpeggios within the notes of the scale. The notes of the 7th arpeggio are displayed in grey, the root of the arpeggio in black and the remaining scale notes in white.

◦ 7th Arpeggio

○ Scale or mode

● Root of the 7th arpeggio

Vertical Harmonized Scale

As with the major scale, the harmonized melodic minor scale is displayed in two sections; the vertical harmonized scale and horizontal harmonized scale.

The first of the two is the vertical harmonized scale which is displayed by utilizing all five patterns of the CAGED system and laying out the seven arpeggios that stem from each scale degree of the melodic minor scale. For example, take the CAGED system's pattern 1 of the melodic minor scale. That pattern is portrayed at the top of the page and below it appears the same pattern of the scale, but on each of the seven diagrams there is a different arpeggio that is built from a different scale degree.

Remember to practice this is in all of the keys of the melodic minor scale.

Scale Patterns

Vertical Harmonized Melodic Minor Scale (Pattern 1)

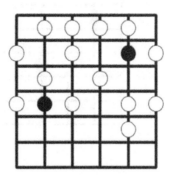

Im(maj7)   IIm7   bIIImaj7(#5)   IV7

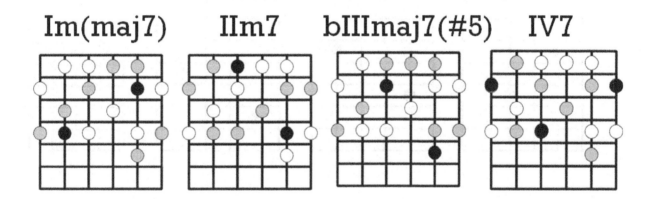

V7   VIm7(b5)   VIIm7(b5)

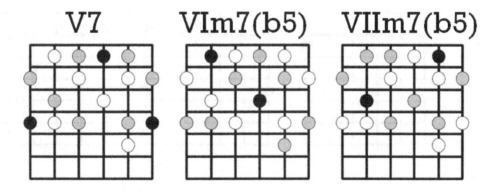

Vertical Harmonized Melodic Minor Scale (Pattern 2)

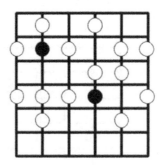

Im(maj7) IIm7 bIIImaj7(#5) IV7

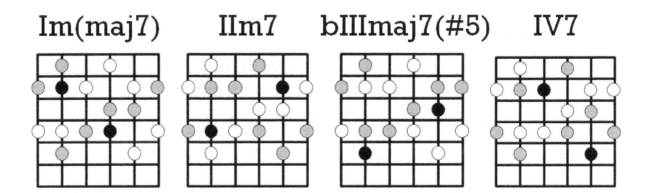

V7 VIm7(b5) VIIm7(b5)

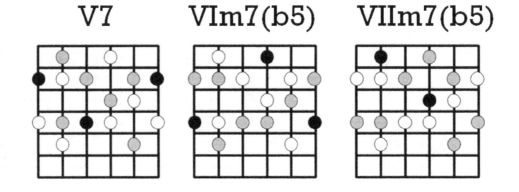

Vertical Harmonized Melodic Minor Scale (Pattern 3)

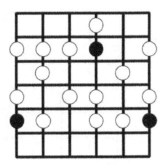

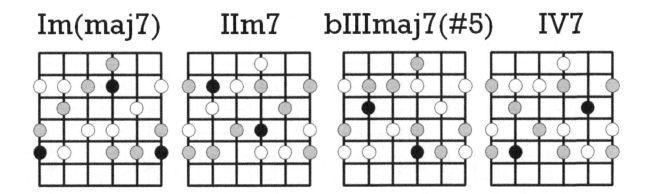

Im(maj7)   IIm7   bIIImaj7(#5)   IV7

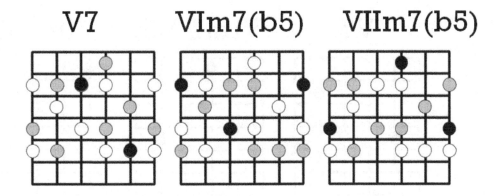

V7   VIm7(b5)   VIIm7(b5)

Vertical Harmonized Melodic Minor Scale (Pattern 4)

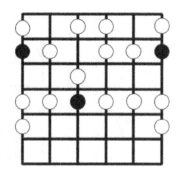

Im(maj7)   IIm7   bIIImaj7(#5)   IV7

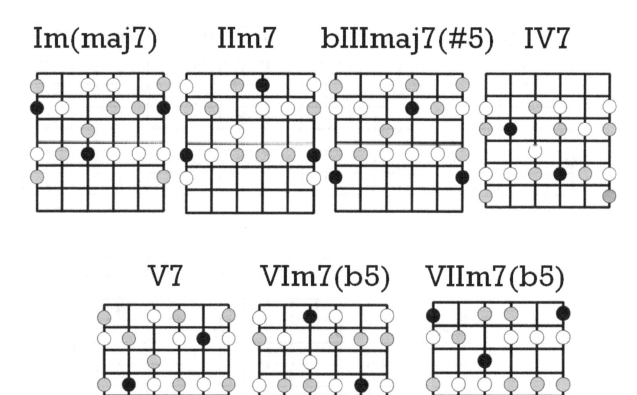

V7   VIm7(b5)   VIIm7(b5)

Vertical Harmonized Melodic Minor Scale (Pattern 5)

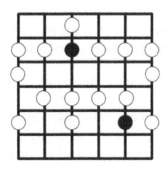

Im(maj7) IIm7 bIIImaj7(#5) IV7

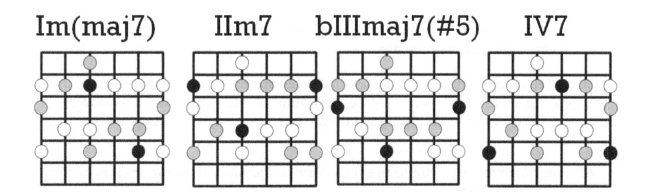

V7 VIm7(b5) VIIm7(b5)

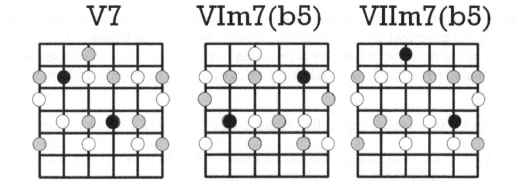

Exercise and Application

- Learn the harmonized scale order

Learn all five CAGED scale patterns with their seven respective arpeggios in their order (play the Im(maj7) arpeggio, followed by the IIm7, then the bIIImaj7(#5) and so on until you reach the octave). You can use a metronome once familiarized with the patterns to create fluidity and cleanness.

- Practice shifting between specific arpeggios and the scale

You can practice each arpeggio on their own and how they feel as you shift between the scale and that one specific arpeggio. This is to be repeated on all of the five positions of the CAGED pattern and all seven of the arpeggios of the scale.

Also practice shifting between all seven arpeggios and the notes of the scale.

- Practice weaving the harmonized melodic minor scale with the harmonized major scale

Since the melodic minor scale and its modes are commonly used to spice up things here and there instead of being a main tonality in a tune; it's good to practice it while interchanging it with the harmonized major scale where possible.

Although I encourage you to use it as the main tonality if you wish (it is one of my personal favorites).

- Practice over Jazz Standards and other tunes

Apply the arpeggios and scales over your favorite jazz standards and tunes to add a more practical approach to practicing the material in the book. Follow the chords of the tunes with just the arpeggios over one of the CAGED scale patterns. You can also practice flowing/shifting between the arpeggios and scales over the same tunes.

This is to be repeated over all five patterns of the CAGED scale patterns.

It is also important to mix up the harmonized melodic minor scale with other scales (especially the major scale) when practicing over tunes.

- Write your own tunes

Always, always, always try to get creative with new material. Writing music is a great way to use new material in a practical manner while adapting it to your own style.

Horizontal Harmonized Scale

As explained in the harmonized major scale section of the book, the way the horizontal harmonized scale is pictured is by displaying one of the five specific octave shapes of the CAGED system and showing below it, the seven arpeggios that stem from the melodic minor scale on that specific octave. In this case the melodic minor scale has to be visualized as running through the same string.

For example, take the notes in C melodic minor. Let's work on playing that scale up the 5th string. It would look something like this.

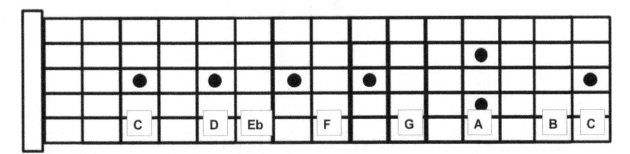

Once having visualized the scale over one string in a horizontal fashion, the next step is to visualize and practice the positioning of both the melodic minor and the seven arpeggios that stem from that scale.

Another way to look at it (in this case) is by starting from the C in the 3rd fret and playing both the arpeggio of the Im(maj7) chord (using the pattern 1 octave of the CAGED system) and the melodic minor scale pattern over which that arpeggio appears. Next go to the D note in the 5th and play both the arpeggio of the IIm7 chord (using the pattern 1 octave of the CAGED system) and the melodic minor scale pattern over which that arpeggio appears. Then keep repeating this process until you complete the scale by reaching the C note at the 15th fret.

This process is to be repeated on all 5 octaves of the CAGED system, all 6 strings of the instrument and all twelve keys of the melodic minor scale.

Horizontal Harmonized Melodic Minor Scale (Pattern 1)

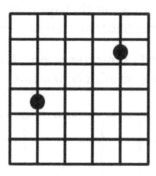

Im(maj7)　　IIm7　　bIIImaj7(#5)　　IV7

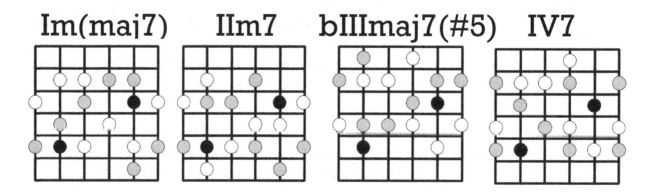

V7　　VIm7(b5)　　VIIm7(b5)

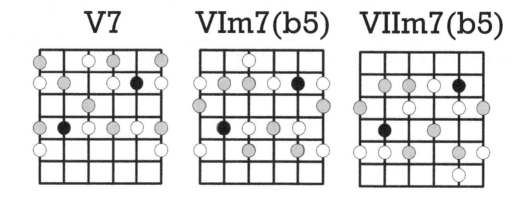

Horizontal Harmonized Melodic Minor Scale (Pattern 2)

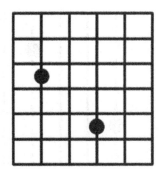

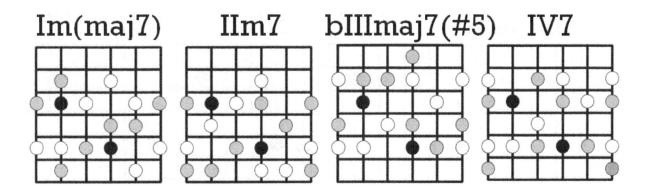

Im(maj7)   IIm7   bIIImaj7(#5)   IV7

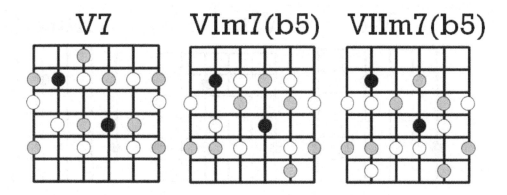

V7   VIm7(b5)   VIIm7(b5)

Horizontal Harmonized Melodic Minor Scale (Pattern 3)

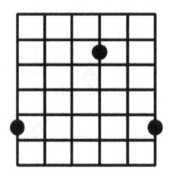

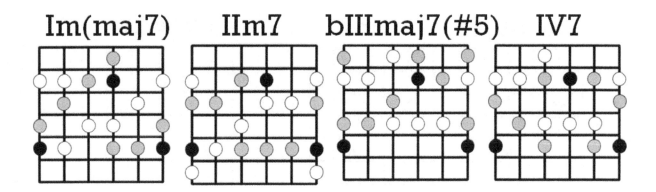

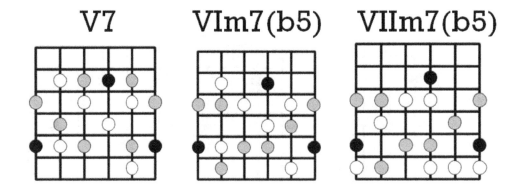

Horizontal Harmonized Melodic Minor Scale (Pattern 4)

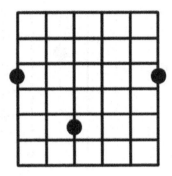

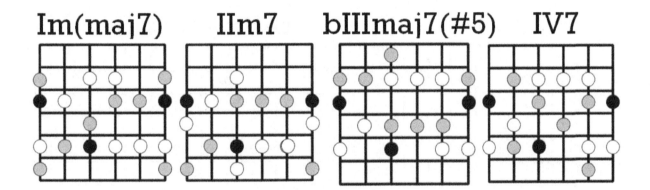

Im(maj7)   IIm7   bIIImaj7(#5)   IV7

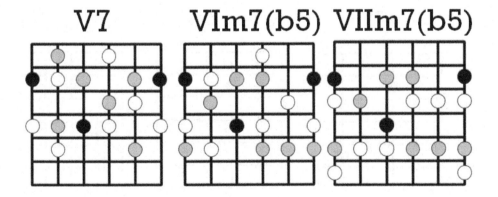

V7   VIm7(b5)   VIIm7(b5)

Horizontal Harmonized Melodic Minor Scale (Pattern 5)

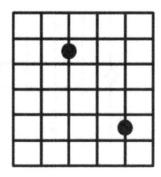

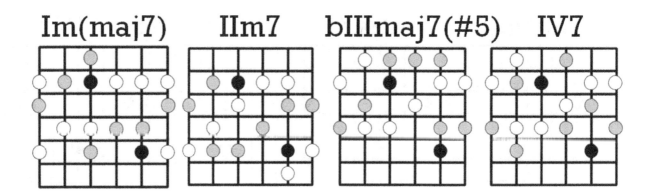

Im(maj7)   IIm7   bIIImaj7(#5)   IV7

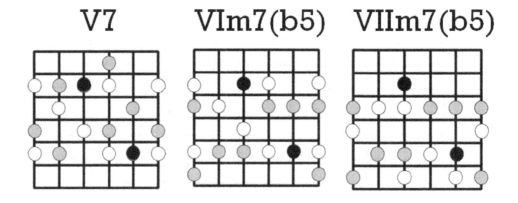

V7   VIm7(b5)   VIIm7(b5)

Exercise and Application

- Learn the harmonized scale order

Learn all 7 arpeggios in order over the same string root. Play the Im(maj7) arpeggio, followed by the IIm7, then the bIIImaj7(#5) and so on until you reach the octave. This time you will be sticking to the same CAGED octave for each of the seven arpeggios. This means that the actual scale patterns will be shifting on just about every new arpeggio. You can use a metronome once familiarized with the patterns to create fluidity and cleanness.

- Practice shifting between specific arpeggios and the scale

You can practice each arpeggio on their own and how they feel as you shift between the scale and that one specific arpeggio. This is to be repeated on all seven of the arpeggios of the scale and all five octaves of the CAGED pattern system.

Also practice shifting between the seven arpeggios and the notes of the scale.

- Practice weaving the harmonized melodic minor scale mixed with the harmonized major scale.

Having the ability of changing between the major scale and the melodic minor scale is something essential when trying to spice up your sound. It's a great way to make things a bit more interesting.

- Practice over Jazz Standards and other tunes

Apply the arpeggios and scale over your favorite jazz standards and/or any other tune to add a more practical approach of the material. Follow the chords of the tunes with just the arpeggios over one of the strings on the guitar.

You can also practice flowing/shifting between the arpeggios and scales over the same tunes.

This is to be repeated over all five patterns of the CAGED scale patterns.

- Transcribe your favorite players and relate the playing to the material

Transcribe and learn solos from your favorite players. Analyze what they are playing and relate the information behind the solos to the information given in the book. Where do they play a straight up arpeggio? Where do they play the scale? Where do they weave both together? Do they begin their lines mostly with the arpeggio or the scale? How do they resolve their lines? What are their tendencies?

3. Pentatonic Scale Weaving

The pentatonic scales used in this section of the book are one in the same with the ones utilized for the scale packs section. If there is any doubt on how these scales were obtained you should re-visit the pentatonic section of the melodic minor scale packs section of the book. There is a thorough explanation and some examples of the full process of pentatonic modification.

Now, it is more common to view the major scale and its modes in this pentatonic weaving perspective of adding notes to the pentatonic scale to result in a full heptatonic scale. But it is not exclusive to the major scale. So, why not do the same with the rest of the scales in the book? The result is an abundance of pentatonic scales that fit perfectly within these heptatonic scales and modes. This means more pentatonic artillery for your musical arsenal. It also means an abundance of possible signature sounds that can be used in the development of your own personal style.

There is a color code that must be used as a guide as with all the other scale weaving diagrams. In this case the notes of the pentatonic scale are depicted in grey while the rest of the heptatonic scale is depicted in white. The root of both of these scales is depicted as black.

◯ Pentatonic scale

◯ Scale or mode

● Root of the scale

Pentatonic Scale > Heptatonic Scale

Modal Order	Pentatonic Scale	Heptatonic Scale
1	Min(maj7) 1 b3 4 5 7	Melodic Minor 1 2 b3 4 5 6 7
2	Minor 1 b3 4 5 b7	Dorian b2 1 b2 b3 4 5 6 b7
3	Major(#5) 1 2 3 #5 6	Lydian Augmented 1 2 3 #4 #5 6 7
4	Major 1 2 3 5 6	Lydian Dominant 1 2 3 #4 5 6 b7
5	Major(b6) 1 2 3 5 b6	Mixolydian b6 1 2 3 4 5 b6 b7
6	Min7(b5) 1 b3 4 b5 b7	Locrian nat 2 1 2 b3 4 b5 b6 b7
7a	Dom7(b2, b5) 1 b2 3 b5 b7	Altered 1 1 b2 b3 b4 b5 b6 b7 or 1 b2 #2 3 b5 #5 b7
7b	Dom7(#2, #5) 1 #2 3 #5 b7	Altered 2 1 b2 b3 b4 b5 b6 b7 or 1 b2 #2 3 b5 #5 b7
7c	Dom7 (b2, #5) 1 b2 3 #5 b7	Altered 3 1 b2 b3 b4 b5 b6 b7 or 1 b2 #2 3 b5 #5 b7
7d	Dom7(#2, b5) 1 #2 3 b5 b7	Altered 4 1 b2 b3 b4 b5 b6 b7 or 1 b2 #2 3 b5 #5 b7

Scale Diagrams

Melodic Minor w/ Min(maj7) Pentatonic Weaving:

Min(maj7) Pentatonic	Melodic Minor
1 b3 4 5 7	1 2 b3 4 5 6 7

- **Chords to play over: Minor, Min(maj7), Min(maj9), Min(maj11), Min(maj13), etc.**

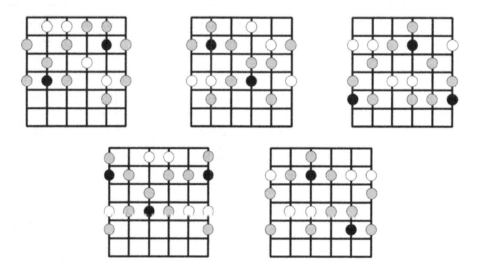

Exercise

A Melodic Minor

Dorian b2 w/ Minor Pentatonic Weaving

Minor Pentatonic	Dorian b2
1 b3 4 5 b7	1 b2 b3 4 5 6 b7

- **Chords to play over: Minor, Min7, Min7(b9), Min11, Min13, etc.**

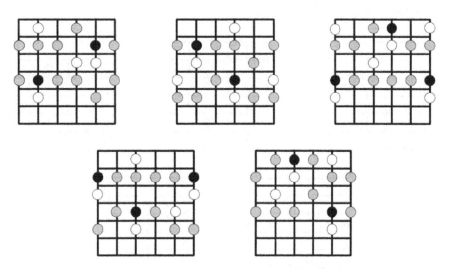

Exercise

Bb Dorian b2

Lydian Augmented w/ Major (#5) Pentatonic Weaving

Major (#5) Pentatonic	Lydian Augmented
1 2 3 #5 6	1 2 3 #4 #5 6 7

- Chords to play over: Augmented tried, Maj7(#5), Maj7(#11, #5), Maj13(#5), etc.

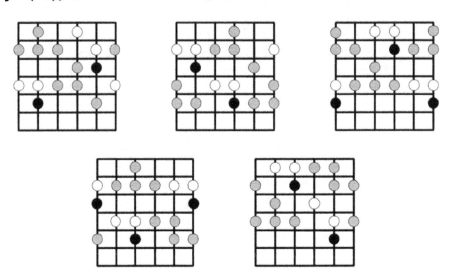

Exercise

F Lydian Augmented

Lydian Dominant w/ Major Pentatonic Weaving

Major Pentatonic	Lydian Dominant
1 2 3 5 6	1 2 3 #4 5 6 b7

- **Chords to play over: Major, Dom7, Dom9, Dom7(#11), Dom 13, etc.**

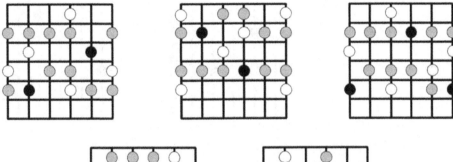

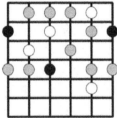 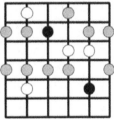

Exercise

G Lydian Dominant

Mixolydian b6 w/ Major (b6) Pentatonic Weaving

Major (b6) Pentatonic	Mixolydian b6
1 2 3 5 b6	1 2 3 4 5 b6 b7

- **Chords to play over: Major, Dom7, Dom9, Dom11, Dom7(b13), etc.**

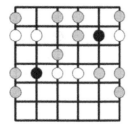 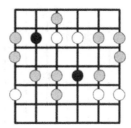 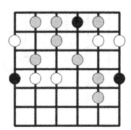

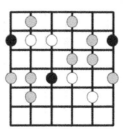 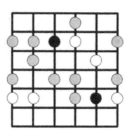

Exercise

D Mixolydian b6

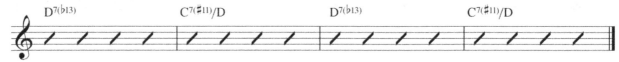

Locrian nat 2 w/ Min7(b5) Pentatonic Weaving

Min7(b5) Pentatonic	Locrian nat 2
1 b3 4 b5 b7	1 2 b3 4 b5 b6 b7

- **Chords to play over: Diminished triad, Min7(b5), Min9(b5), etc.**

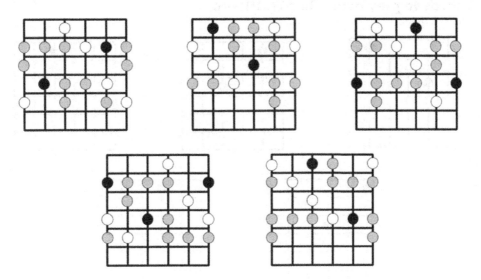

Exercise

Ab Locrian nat 2

Altered w/ Dom7 (b2, b5) Pentatonic Weaving

Dom7(b2,b5) Pentatonic	Altered
1 b2 3 b5 b7	1 b2 b3 b4 b5 b6 b7 1 b2 #2 3 b5 #5 b7

- **Chords to play over: Dom7(alt), etc.**

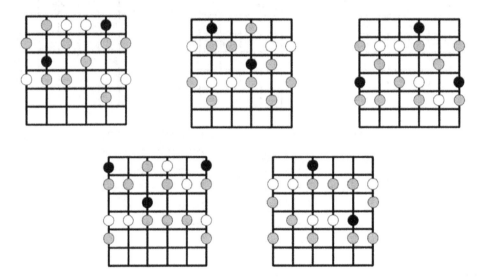

Exercise

C# Altered

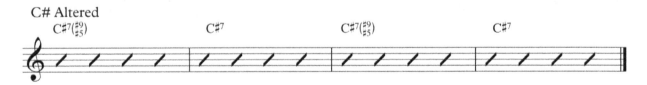

Altered w/ Dom7(#2, #5) Pentatonic Weaving

Dom7(#2,#5) Pentatonic	Altered
1 #2 3 #5 b7	1 b2 b3 b4 b5 b6 b7
	1 b2 #2 3 b5 #5 b7

- **Chords to play over: Dom7(alt), etc.**

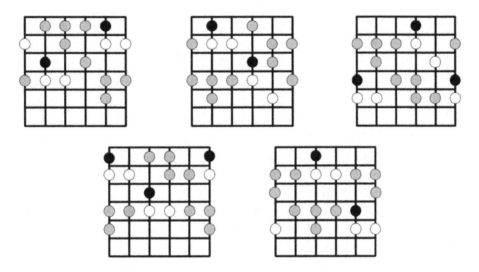

Exercise

A Altered

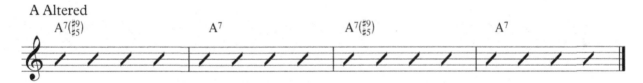

Altered w/ Dom7 (b2, #5) Pentatonic Weaving

Dom7(b2,#5) Pentatonic	Altered
1 b2 3 #5 b7	1 b2 b3 b4 b5 b6 b7
	1 b2 #2 3 b5 #5 b7

- **Chords to play over: Dom7(alt), etc.**

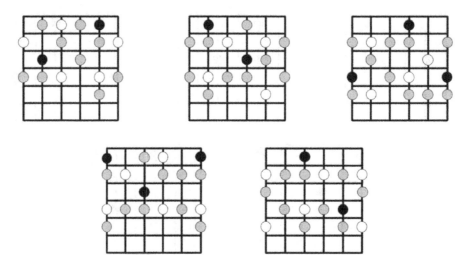

Exercise

Altered w/ Dom7 (#2, b5) Pentatonic Weaving

Dom7(#2,b5) Pentatonic	Altered
1 #2 3 b5 b7	1 b2 b3 b4 b5 b6 b7 1 b2 #2 3 b5 #5 b7

- **Chords to play over: Dom7(alt), etc.**

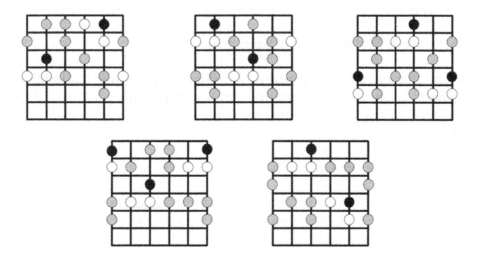

Exercise

B Altered

Exercise and Application

- Experiment with the new material

In the major pentatonic weaving section, we got a glimpse of some new pentatonic scales (specifically the Min7(b5) pentatonic for the Locrian mode). That's exactly what's so cool about the melodic minor pentatonic weaving section; new pentatonic scales. There's a whole bunch of them and it only gets even more interesting as the next few chapters go along. Modified pentatonic scales are a world of their own and I highly suggest experimenting with the ones in the book (and even coming up with some pentatonic scales of your own).

- Create some new material of your own

I have given you guys a hefty number of modified pentatonic scales that can be used as a base to play full on heptatonic scales. But I highly suggest that you get to creating some of your own pentatonic scales which can be based on any scale or mode that you like.

- Learn from the masters

Look for songs, pieces, licks and any piece of music out there by any of your favorite players that incorporate the melodic minor scale. Analyze what they're doing and adapt it to your own music style.

- Write music

I just have to keep mentioning this; write music, songs, licks, exercises, create new phrases and vocabulary using the concepts in the book as your own. The important thing about this material is for you to find a musical purpose for it.

Chapter Three

Harmonic Minor Scale and Modes

The harmonic minor scale can be heard in a wide number of musical genres around the world. From the fast note flurries of neo classical shred, to jazz, classical and the folkloric music of many places around the world, this scale has withstood the test of time. One of the favored modes in this scale is definitely the Phrygian Dominant mode which can be heard over tons of neo classical solos and V chords in minor II-V-I progressions.

The whole tone (W)/half tone (H) formula for this scale is W H W W H W+H H. As you can probably tell there is something completely new within this scale. This is the W+H step within the b6th and 7th degrees of the scale. This is the union of a whole tone and a half tone to create a distance of a step and a half (also called a minor 3rd).

As far as the intervallic formula for this scale we have 1 2 b3 4 5 b6 7.

The most popular modes within the harmonic minor scale are Phrygian Dominant and the root mode itself (harmonic minor). Although some of the other propositions of this scale are just as interesting. And being that they are not as commonly used as these popular modes you might just find an out of the box sound that you could use to define your own specific style.

Below is a table with the scale name, intervallic formula, W/H formula and root chord of each mode within the harmonic minor scale.

Scale Name	Intervallic Formula	W/H Formula	Root Chord
Harmonic Minor	1 2 b3 4 5 b6 7	W H W W H (W+H) H	Min(maj7)
Locrian nat 6	1 b2 b3 4 b5 6 b7	H W W H (W+H) H W	Min7(b5)
Ionian #5	1 2 3 4 #5 6 7	W W H (W+H) H W H	Maj7(#5)
Dorian #4	1 2 b3 #4 5 6 b7	W H (W+H) H W H W	Min7
Phrygian Dominant	1 b2 3 4 5 b6 b7	H (W+H) H W H W W	Dom7
Lydian #2	1 #2 3 #4 5 6 7	(W+H) H W H W W H	Maj7
Altered bb7	1 b2 b3 b4 b5 b6 bb7	H W H W W H (W+H)	Dim7

It is important to have a good grasp of the name, intervallic formula and root chord of each of these modes so that you may fully understand the application of the concepts to come. The whole tone/half tone formula is not such an essential category as the other categories within the table (in a practical purpose), but it does not hurt to have an understanding of this as well.

1. Harmonic Minor Scale Packs (triad/pentatonic/heptatonic)

Triad

When it comes to the harmonic minor scale, we are right back down to the 4 basic types of triads; major, minor, augmented and diminished.

Major	Minor	Augmented	Diminished
1 3 5	1 b3 5	1 3 #5	1 b3 b5

Pentatonic

After going through the same process of pentatonic scale modification explained in the melodic minor section of the book, we end up with even more new pentatonic scales for the harmonic minor scale. Yes, we find some of the same pentatonic as in the melodic minor scale like the Min(maj7) pentatonic and the Min7(b5) pentatonic. But there are a couple of new pentatonic modifications in the mix.

Pentatonic Scale	Intervallic Construction	Pentatonic Scale	Intervallic Construction
Min7(#11) Pentatonic	1 b3 #4 5 b7	Major(#2) Pentatonic	1 #2 3 5 6
Major(b2, b6) Pentatonic	1 b2 3 5 b6	Diminished(b2) Pentatonic	1 b2 b3 b5 bb7

All the while, always remember to keep the perspective of the pentatonic scale as a triad with two extra added notes.

Triad	2 added notes	Pentatonic Scale
1 b3 5	+ 4, 7	= 1 b3 4 5 7

Heptatonic

Again, the main perspective to have in these scale packs is that of it all being the same material with some minor changes. In the case of the heptatonic scales, it's all a matter of adding two notes to the pentatonic scale already studied. In this case we look at the Min(maj7) pentatonic (1 b3 4 5 7) and add a major 2nd and a b6th resulting in the harmonic minor scale (1 2 b3 4 5 b6 7).

Pentatonic Scale	2 added notes	Harmonic Minor Scale
1 b3 4 5 7	+ 2, b6	= 1 2 b3 4 5 b6 7

This process is repeated with all seven modes of the Harmonic Minor scale.

Triad > Pentatonic Scale > Heptatonic Scale

Triad	Pentatonic Scale	Heptatonic Scale
Minor 1 b3 5	Min(maj7) 1 b3 4 5 7	Harmonic Minor 1 2 b3 4 5 b6 7
Diminished 1 b3 b5	Min7(b5) 1 b3 4 b5 b7	Locrian nat 6 1 b2 b3 4 b5 6 b7
Augmented 1 3 #5	Major(#5) 1 2 3 #5 6	Ionian #5 1 2 3 4 #5 6 7
Minor 1 b3 5	Min7(#11) 1 b3 #4 5 b7	Dorian #4 1 2 b3 #4 5 6 b7
Major 1 3 5	Major(b2, b6) 1 b2 3 5 b6	Phrygian Dominant 1 b2 3 4 5 b6 b7
Major 1 3 5	Major(#2) 1 #2 3 5 6	Lydian #2 1 #2 3 #4 5 6 7
Diminished 1 b3 b5	Diminished(b2) 1 b2 b3 b5 bb7	Altered bb7 1 b2 b3 b4 b5 b6 bb7

Scale Diagrams

Harmonic Minor Scale Pack

Minor Triad	Min(maj7) Pentatonic	Harmonic Minor
1 b3 5	1 b3 4 5 7	1 2 b3 4 5 b6 7

Pattern 1

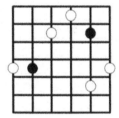
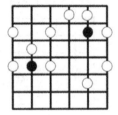
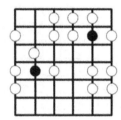

Pattern 2

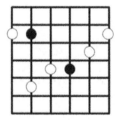
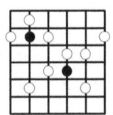
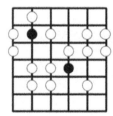

Pattern 3

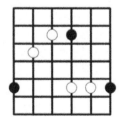
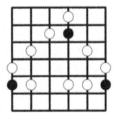
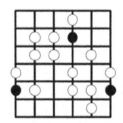

Pattern 4

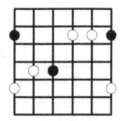 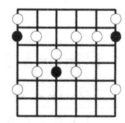 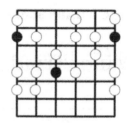

Pattern 5

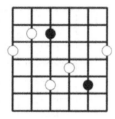 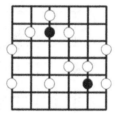 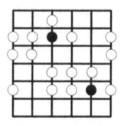

Exercise

Ab Harmonic Minor

Abm(maj7)   Eb7(b9)   Abm(maj7)   Eb7(b9)

Locrian nat 6 Scale Pack

Diminished Triad	Min7(b5) Pentatonic	Locrian nat 6
1 b3 b5	1 b3 4 b5 b7	1 b2 b3 4 b5 6 b7

Pattern 1

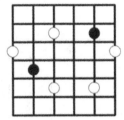 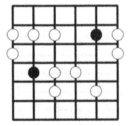 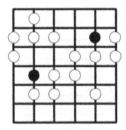

Pattern 2

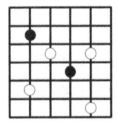 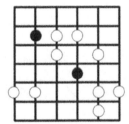 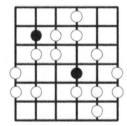

Pattern 3

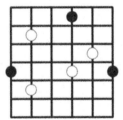 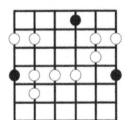 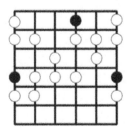

Pattern 4

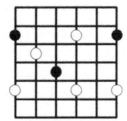 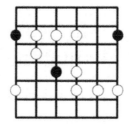 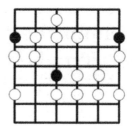

Pattern 5

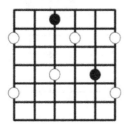 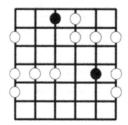 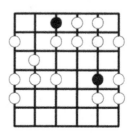

Exercise

Bb Locrian nat 6

Ionian #5 Scale Pack

Augmented Triad	Major (#5) Pentatonic	Ionian #5
1 3 #5	1 2 3 #5 6	1 2 3 4 #5 6 7

Pattern 1

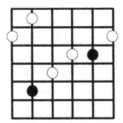 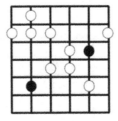 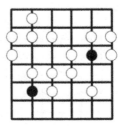

Pattern 2

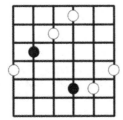 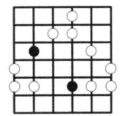 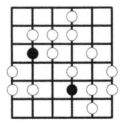

Pattern 3

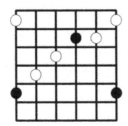 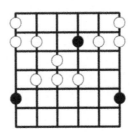 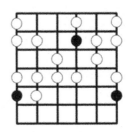

Pattern 4

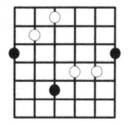 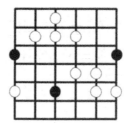 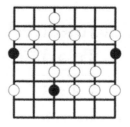

Pattern 5

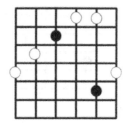 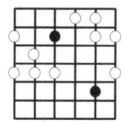 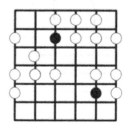

Exercise

C Ionian #5

Dorian #4 Scale Pack

Minor Triad	Minor (#4) Pentatonic	Dorian #4
1 b3 5	1 b3 #4 5 b7	1 2 b3 #4 5 6 b7

Pattern 1

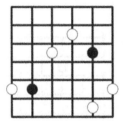 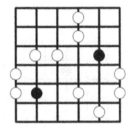 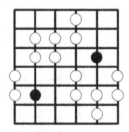

Pattern 2

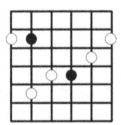 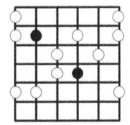 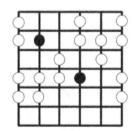

Pattern 3

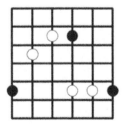 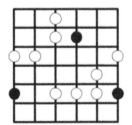 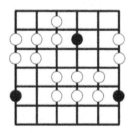

Pattern 4

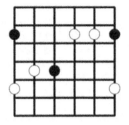 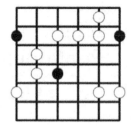 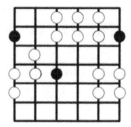

Pattern 5

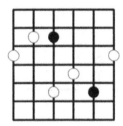 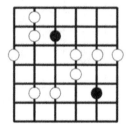 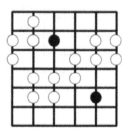

Exercise

G Dorian #4

Phrygian Dominant Scale Packs

Major Triad	Major (b2, b6) Pentatonic	Phrygian Dominant
1 3 5	1 b2 3 5 b6	1 b2 3 4 5 b6 b7

Pattern 1

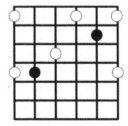 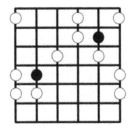 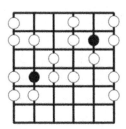

Pattern 2

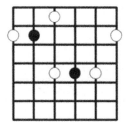 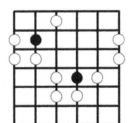 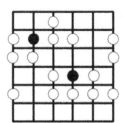

Pattern 3

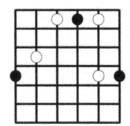 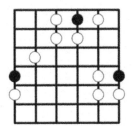 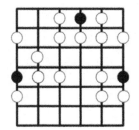

Pattern 4

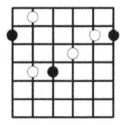 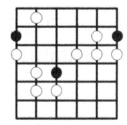 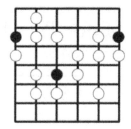

Pattern 5

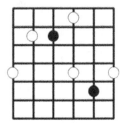 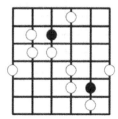 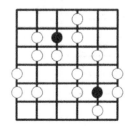

Exercise

Eb Phrygian Dominant

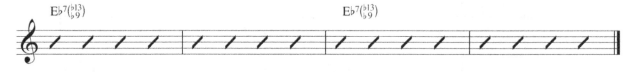

Lydian #2 Scale Pack

Major Triad	Major (#2) Pentatonic	Lydian #2
1 3 5	1 #2 3 5 6	1 #2 3 #4 5 6 7

Pattern 1

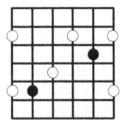 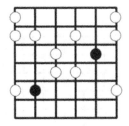 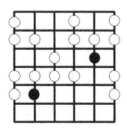

Pattern 2

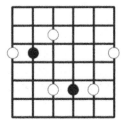 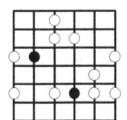 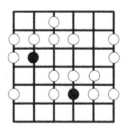

Pattern 3

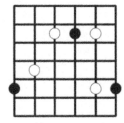 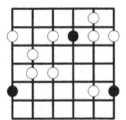 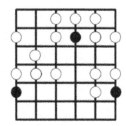

Pattern 4

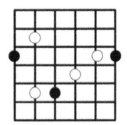 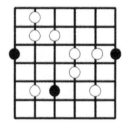 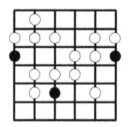

Pattern 5

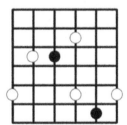 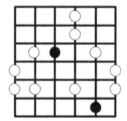 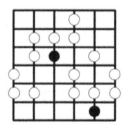

Exercise

C Lydian #2

Altered bb7 Scale Packs

Diminished Triad	Diminished (b2) Pentatonic	Altered bb7
1 b3 b5	1 b2 b3 b5 bb7	1 b2 b3 b4 b5 b6 bb7

Pattern 1

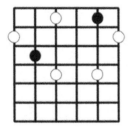 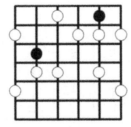 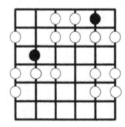

Pattern 2

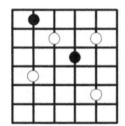 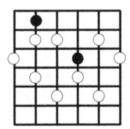 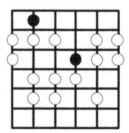

Pattern 3

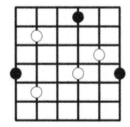 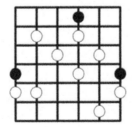 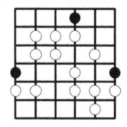

Pattern 4

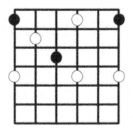 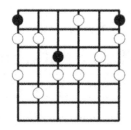 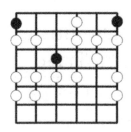

Pattern 5

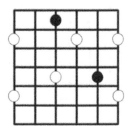 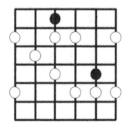 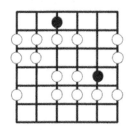

Exercise

E Altered bb7

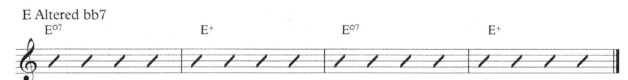

Exercise and Application

- Don't forget the basics

Don't think for a second that triads are less important because they have fewer notes than the pentatonic and heptatonic scales. You will need to target those triad notes when you start playing around with chord tones. They are also great for coming up with interesting rhythm guitar parts.

Practice improvising and creating melodies using only triads. Use them individually, combine them and get creative with them. Make triads a staple of your playing.

- Pick and choose

It's natural that you will enjoy some sounds more than others so take note on which of these triads, pentatonic scales and heptatonic scales you enjoy the most. Make a list of your favorite sounds and make sure to revisit them consistently while practicing.

- Experiment with the phrasing

Don't just play the material up and down while the chord progression is playing in the background; play around with different combinations of these notes. Try different note groupings, intervals, note orderings, repeatable phrases. Make the exercises as creative and musical as you can.

- Use it in real life

Don't just leave this new information in the woodshed; use your brand new skills out in the real world. Apply the new triads, pentatonic and heptatonic scales in your solos and rhythm guitar parts on your next gig, jam and/or rehearsal.

2. Harmonized Scale Weaving

After stacking all seven scale degrees of the harmonic minor scale in thirds; you are left with the specific 7th chords that pertain to each degree of the scale. Below is an example of this using the C harmonic minor scale.

Below is a table demonstrating all seven chords using roman numerals to identify each scale degree. As with all scales, it's good to visualize them as roman numerals for transposition purposes.

Harmonized Harmonic Minor Scale						
Im(maj7)	IIm7(b5)	bIIImaj7(#5)	IVm7	V7	bVImaj7	VII°7

All the while the same process of scale weaving is put in play to help with the visualization of the seven arpeggios within the harmonic minor scale. This is done by showing the notes of the 7th arpeggios in grey, the root of such arpeggios in black and the rest of the notes within the scale in white.

⬤ 7th Arpeggio

○ Scale or mode

● Root of the 7th arpeggio

Vertical Harmonized Scale

The vertical harmonized scale is displayed by utilizing all five patterns of the CAGED system and laying out the seven arpeggios that stem from each scale degree of the harmonic minor scale. For example, take the CAGED system's pattern 1 of the harmonic minor scale. That pattern is portrayed at the top of the page while underneath it appears the same pattern of the scale, but on each of the seven diagrams there is a different arpeggio that is built from a different scale degree.

Remember to practice this is in all of the keys of the harmonic minor scale.

Scale Diagrams

Vertical Harmonized Harmonic Minor Scale (Pattern 1)

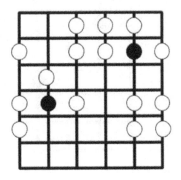

Im(maj7)   IIm7(b5)   bIIImaj7(#5)   IVm7

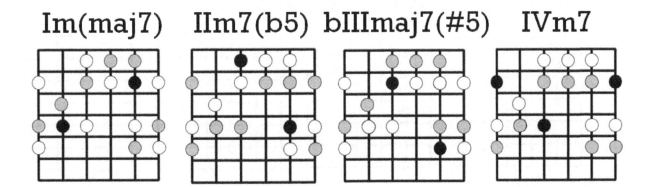

V7   bVImaj7   VII°7

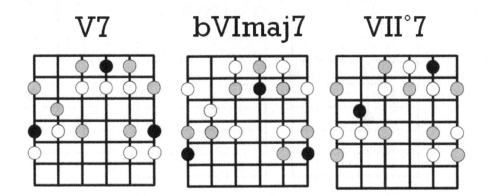

Vertical Harmonized Harmonic Minor Scale (Pattern 2)

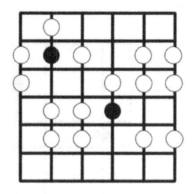

Im(maj7) IIm7(b5) bIIImaj7(#5)   IVm7

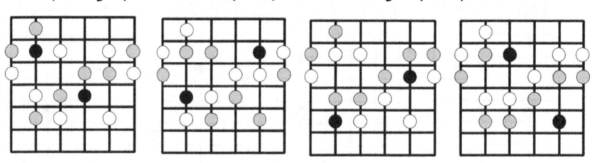

V7   bVImaj7   VII°7

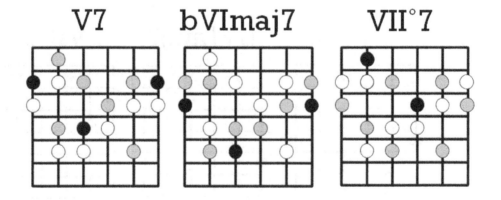

Vertical Harmonized Harmonic Minor Scale (Pattern 3)

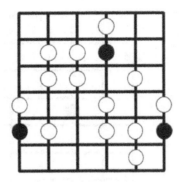

Im(maj7)   IIm7(b5)   bIIImaj7(#5)   IVm7

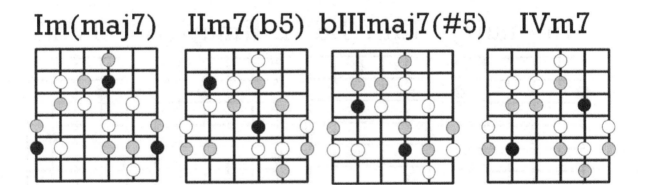

V7   bVImaj7   VII°7

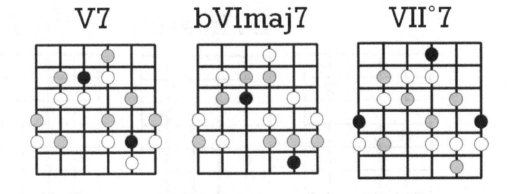

Vertical Harmonized Harmonic Minor Scale (Pattern 4)

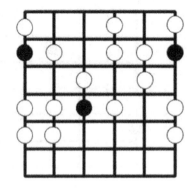

Im(maj7)   IIm7(b5)   bIIImaj7(#5)   IVm7

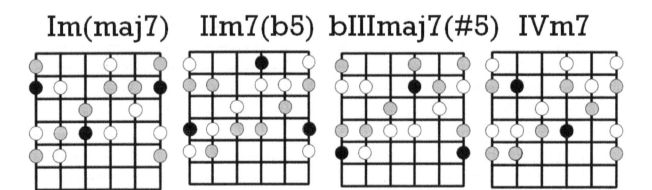

V7   bVImaj7   VII°7

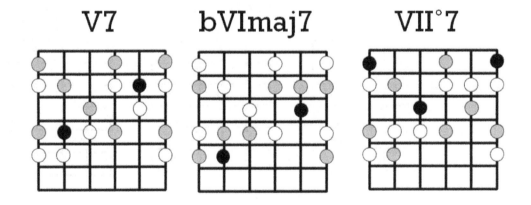

Vertical Harmonized Harmonic Minor Scale (Pattern 5)

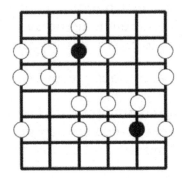

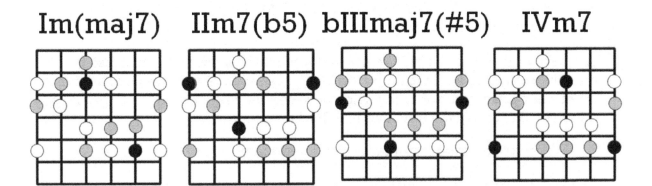

Im(maj7)   IIm7(b5)   bIIImaj7(#5)   IVm7

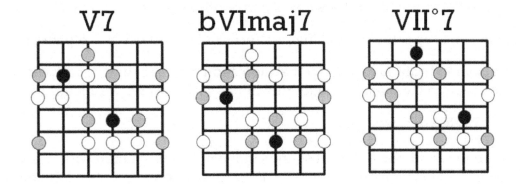

V7   bVImaj7   VII°7

Exercise and Application

- Learn the harmonized scale order

Learn all five CAGED scale patterns with their seven respective arpeggios in their order. So play the Im(maj7) arpeggio, followed by the IIm7(b5), then the bIIImaj7(#5) and so on until you reach the octave. You can use a metronome once familiarized with the patterns to create fluidity and cleanness.

- Practice shifting between specific arpeggios and the scale

You can practice each arpeggio on their own and how they feel as you shift between the scale and that one specific arpeggio. This is to be repeated on all five positions of the CAGED system and all seven of the arpeggios of the scale.

Also practice shifting between the seven arpeggios and the notes of the scale.

- Practice weaving the harmonized harmonic minor scale with the harmonized major scale

The harmonic minor is a bit like the melodic minor scale in that it is also frequently used to make things a bit more interesting in certain areas of a tune. So it is very important to be able to switch between playing harmonic minor and any other scale at any given time and in a fluid manner.

- Practice over Jazz Standards and other tunes

Apply the arpeggios and scale over your favorite jazz standards and/or any other tune to add a more practical approach of the material. Follow the chords of the tunes with just the arpeggios over one of the CAGED scale patterns. You can also practice flowing/shifting between the arpeggios and scales over the same tunes.

This is to be repeated over all five patterns of the CAGED scale patterns.

It is also important to mix up the harmonized harmonic minor scale with other scales such as the major and melodic minor scales when practicing over tunes.

- Write your own tunes

Get creative with the different sounds that can be summoned with this scale and write some tunes, etudes, exercises, licks and/or anything else that you might think of. It's a great tool for in the musician's toolbox.

Horizontal Harmonized Scale

By now you should already be familiarized with how the scales and arpeggios are displayed and know that one of the key pieces of information to understanding the harmonized scale is to know your scales in a horizontal fashion. In other words, you have to be able to play the scale on just one string.

For example, take the notes in C harmonic minor. Let's work on playing that scale up the 5th string. It would look something like this.

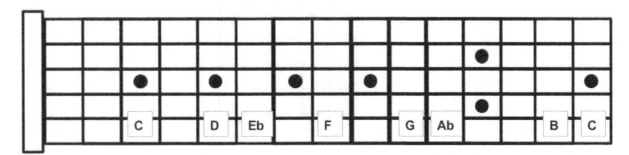

Once having visualized the scale over one string in a horizontal fashion, the next step is to visualize and practice the positioning of both the harmonic minor scale and the seven arpeggios that stem from each of its scale degrees.

Another way to look at it (in this case) is by starting from the C in the 3rd fret and playing both the arpeggio of the Im(maj7) chord (using the pattern 1 octave of the CAGED system) and the harmonic minor scale pattern over which that arpeggio appears. Next go to the D note in the 5th fret and play both the arpeggio of the IIm7(b5) chord (using the pattern 1 octave of the CAGED system) and the harmonic minor scale pattern over which that arpeggio appears. Then keep repeating this process until you complete the scale by reaching the C note at the 15th fret.

This process is to be repeated on all five octaves of the CAGED system, all six strings of the instrument and all twelve keys of the harmonic minor scale.

Scale Diagrams

Horizontal Harmonized Harmonic Minor Scale (Pattern 1)

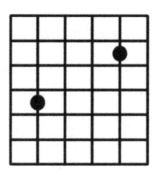

Im(maj7)   IIm7(b5)   bIIImaj7(#5)   IVm7

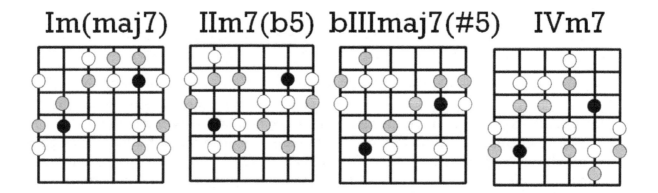

V7   bVImaj7   VII°7

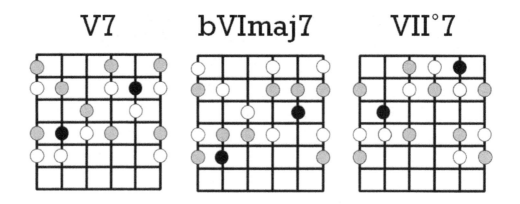

Horizontal Harmonized Harmonic Minor Scale (Pattern 2)

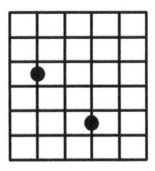

Im(maj7)   IIm7(b5)   bIIImaj7(#5)   IVm7

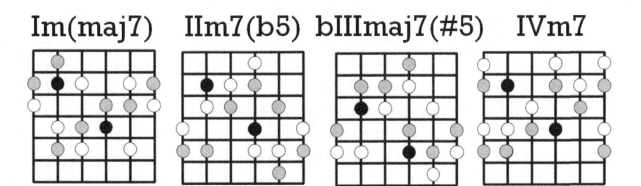

V7   bVImaj7   VII°7

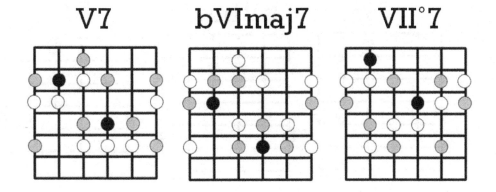

Horizontal Harmonized Harmonic Minor Scale (Pattern 3)

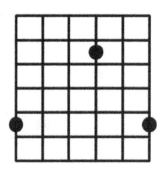

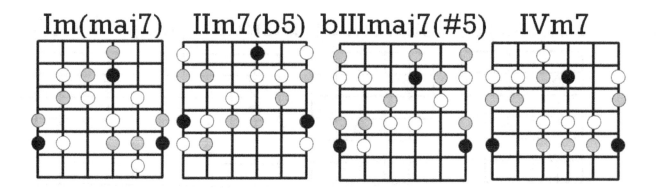

Im(maj7)   IIm7(b5)   bIIImaj7(#5)   IVm7

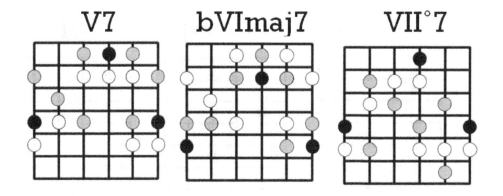

V7   bVImaj7   VII°7

Horizontal Harmonized Harmonic Minor Scale (Pattern 4)

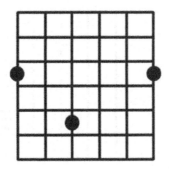

Im(maj7)   IIm7(b5)   bIIImaj7(#5)   IVm7

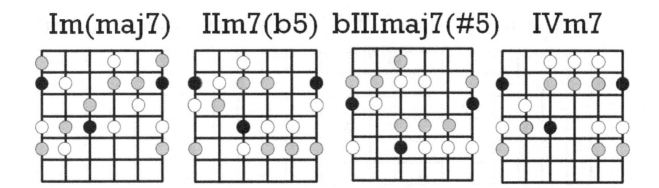

V7   bVImaj7   VII°7

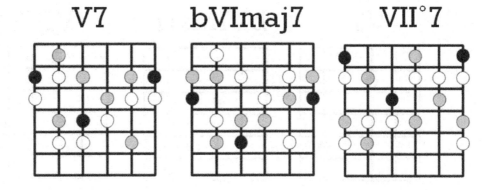

Horizontal Harmonized Harmonic Minor Scale (Pattern 5)

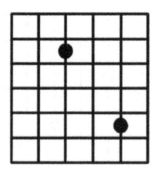

Im(maj7)   IIm7(b5)   bIIImaj7(#5)   IVm7

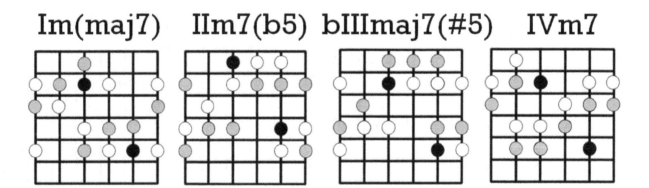

V7   bVImaj7   VII°7

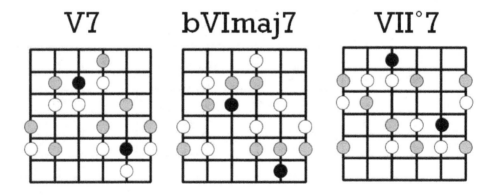

Exercise and Application

- Learn the harmonized scale order

Learn all seven arpeggios in order over the same string root. Play the Im(maj7) arpeggio, followed by the IIm7(b5), then the bIIImaj7(#5) and so on until you reach the octave. This time you will be sticking to the same CAGED octave for the arpeggios. This means that the actual scale patterns will be shifting on just about every new arpeggio. You can use a metronome once familiarized with the patterns to create fluidity and cleanness.

- Practice shifting between specific arpeggios and the scale

You can practice each arpeggio on their own and how they feel as you shift between the scale and that one specific arpeggio. This is to be repeated on all seven of the arpeggios of the scale and all five octaves of the CAGED system.

Also practice shifting between the seven arpeggios and the notes of the scale.

- Practice weaving the harmonized harmonic minor scale mixed with the harmonized major scale.

This ability is invaluable when playing jazz, fusion, progressive rock and many more styles. It is also a great way to developing a signature sound once you start picking and choosing a specific sound palate that better suites the interests of your ear.

- Practice over Jazz Standards and other tunes

Apply the arpeggios and scales over your favorite jazz standards and/or any other tune to add a more practical approach of the material. Follow the chords of the tunes with just the arpeggios over one of the strings on the guitar.

You can also practice flowing/shifting between the arpeggios and scales over the same tunes.

This is to be repeated over all five patterns of the CAGED scale patterns.

- Write your own tunes

Always be creative with new material, it's the best way to easily adapt it to your own vocabulary and playing style. It's also a great way to absorb new ideas into your compositions.

3. Pentatonic Scale Weaving

It's interesting to see how many pentatonic scales arise from within these heptatonic scales. It's also interesting the different sound qualities that these different pentatonic scales have. Some of them have a peculiar sound that tends to reference different ethnicities; others sound incredibly modern and avant-garde to a certain point. Who knew that you could access so many different sounds hidden within these scales by just altering a scale degree or two?

As far as the diagrams go, the notes of the pentatonic scale are depicted in grey while the rest of the heptatonic scale is depicted in white. The root of both of these scales is depicted as black.

◉ Pentatonic scale

○ Scale or mode

● Root of the scale

Pentatonic Scale > Heptatonic Scale

Modal Order	Pentatonic Scale	Heptatonic Scale
1	Min(maj7) 1 b3 4 5 7	Harmonic Minor 1 2 b3 4 5 b6 7
2	Min7(b5) 1 b3 4 b5 b7	Locrian nat 6 1 b2 b3 4 b5 6 b7
3	Major(#5) 1 2 3 #5 6	Ionian #5 1 2 3 4 #5 6 7
4	Min7(#11) 1 b3 #4 5 b7	Dorian #4 1 2 b3 #4 5 6 b7
5	Major(b2, b6) 1 b2 3 5 b6	Phrygian Dominant 1 b2 3 4 5 b6 b7
6	Major(#2) 1 #2 3 5 6	Lydian #2 1 #2 3 #4 5 6 7
7	Diminished(b2) 1 b2 b3 b5 bb7	Altered bb7 1 b2 b3 b4 b5 b6 bb7

Scale Diagrams

Harmonic Minor w/ Min(maj7) Pentatonic Weaving

Min(maj7) Pentatonic	Harmonic Minor
1 b3 4 5 7	1 2 b3 4 5 b6 7

- **Chords to play over: Minor, Min(maj7), Min(maj9), Min(maj11), Min(maj7)(b13), etc.**

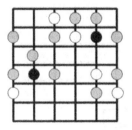 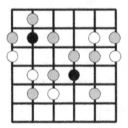 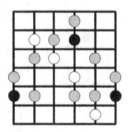

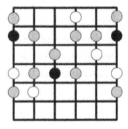 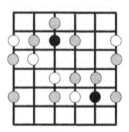

Exercise

C Harmonic Minor

Locrian nat 6 w/ Min7(b5) Pentatonic Weaving

Min7(b5) Pentatonic	Locrian nat 6
1 b3 4 b5 b7	1 b2 b3 4 b5 6 b7

- **Chords to play over: Diminished triad, Min7(b5), Min7(b9, b5), Min13(b5), etc.**

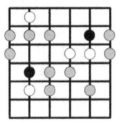 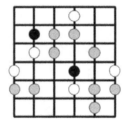 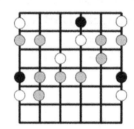

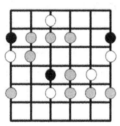 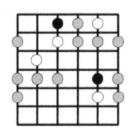

Exercise

Bb Locrian nat 6

Ionian (#5) w/ Major (#5) Pentatonic Weaving

Major (#5) Pentatonic	Ionian #5
1 2 3 #5 6	1 2 3 4 #5 6 7

- **Chords to play over: Augmented triad, Maj7(#5), Maj13(#5), etc.**

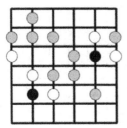 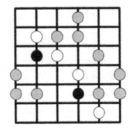 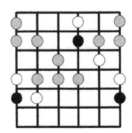

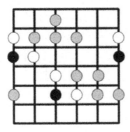 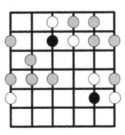

Exercise

D Ionian #5

Dorian #4 w/ Minor (#4) Pentatonic Weaving

Minor (#4) Pentatonic	Dorian #4
1 b3 #4 5 b7	1 2 b3 #4 5 6 b7

- **Chords to play over: Minor, Min7, Min9, Min7(#11), Min13, etc.**

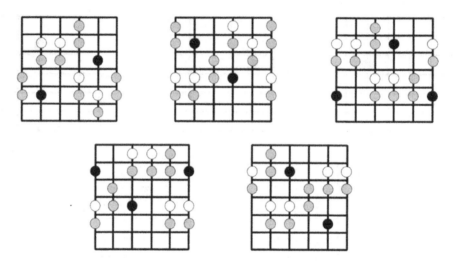

Exercise

Ab Dorian #4

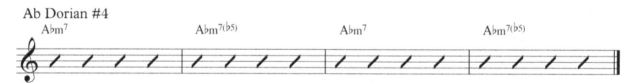

Phrygian Dominant w/ Major (b2, b6) Pentatonic Weaving

Major (b2, b6) Pentatonic	Phrygian Dominant
1 b2 3 5 b6	1 b2 3 4 5 b6 b7

- **Chords to play over: Major, Dom7, Dom7(b9), Dom7(b13), etc.**

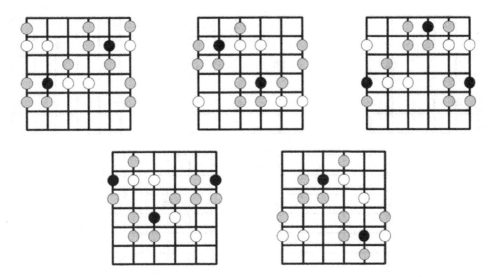

Exercise

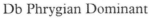

Db Phrygian Dominant

Lydian #2 w/ Major (#2) Pentatonic Weaving

Major (#2) Pentatonic	Lydian #2
1 #2 3 5 6	1 #2 3 #4 5 6 7

- **Chords to play over: Major, Maj7, Maj7(#9), Maj7(#11), Maj13, etc.**

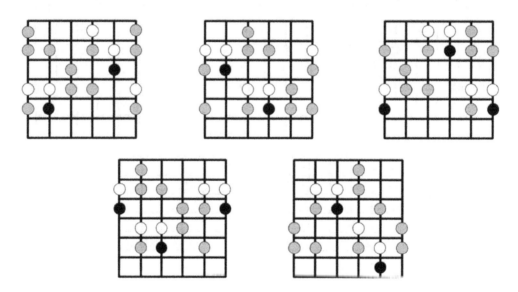

Exercise

G Lydian #2

Altered bb7 w/ Diminished (b2) Pentatonic Weaving

Diminished (b2) Pentatonic	Altered bb7
1 b2 b3 b5 bb7	1 b2 b3 b4 b5 b6 bb7

- **Chords to play over: Dim7, etc.**

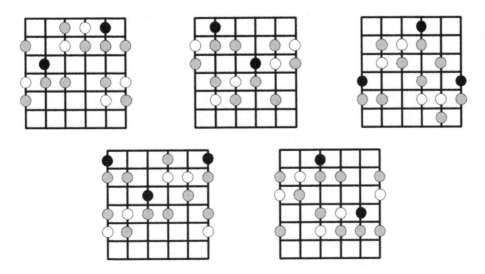

Exercise

F Altered bb7

Exercise and Application

- Learn the material

I haven't mentioned this in the last couple of chapters but it is imperative that you learn the material given for you to obtain results. And when I say learn, I mean to such a degree that you don't have to consciously think about it when you play. It should just flow out of your fingers.

Another important piece of information to be conscious of is that a lot of the material is actually repeated in various sections of the book. By learning the Minor, Major, Min(maj7) and Min7(b5) pentatonic scales, you are learning key core information that is used in various parts of the book.

- Practice going in and out

The sole purpose of the pentatonic weaving concept is to visualize the pentatonic scales that lie within the heptatonic scales. This helps you to have a greater understanding of music in itself, widens your vocabulary and helps you in your path to becoming a better musician.

- Get creative

Look for different ways to apply the information. Try to be as thorough as possible when studying. Create new exercises and practice routines. Try to find as many applications as you can; if you can find a limit number of possibilities for repetitive patterns, permutations, octaves, whatever, then do it. You'll learn more for it and you'll see yourself achieving the results that you want.

Chapter Four

Harmonic Major Scale and Modes

The harmonic major scale is probably the least known of the four main heptatonic scales mentioned in the book. This scale has been known to make appearances in jazz and fusion circles. Especially in today's constantly evolving jazz/fusion scene which is always looking for new sounds and colors to incorporate to their ever expanding vocabulary.

As far as the whole tone/half tone formula for this scale we have W W H W H W+H H. As is with the harmonic minor scale; the harmonic major scale contains a b3 (W+H) interval in between the b6 and 7 scale degrees.

The intervallic build up of this scale is the same as the major scale except for having a b6 instead of the natural 6 found in the major scale. This makes 1 2 3 4 5 b6 7 the intervallic build up for the harmonic major scale.

The harmonic major scale and its modes aren't used as frequently as the other scales mentioned in the book, but it's definitely a must when looking to progress along side by side with some of the newer guitar players out there. They are also a great tool in the expansion on your sonar palate and vocabulary.

As with the some of the not-so-used modes of the harmonic minor scale, you could find a particularly unused color within this scale to base you style around of.

 Even though it's not as popular as its other scalar counterpoints, it's just as important, resourceful and colorful.

Below is a table with the scale name, intervallic formula, W/H formula and root chord of each mode within the harmonic major scale.

Scale Name	Intervallic Formula	W/H Formula	Root Chord
Hamonic Major	1 2 3 4 5 b6 7	W W H W H (W+H) H	Maj7 Or Maj7(#5)/ Maj7(b13)
Dorian b5	1 2 b3 4 b5 6 b7	W H W H (W+H) H W	Min7(b5)
Phrygian b4	1 b2 b3 b4 5 b6 b7 Or 1 b2 #2 3 5 b6 b7	H W H (W+H) H W W	Min7 Or Dom7
Lydian b3	1 2 b3 #4 5 6 7	W H (W+H) H W W H	Min(maj7)
Mixolydian b2	1 b2 3 4 5 6 b7	H (W+H) H W W H W	Dom7
Lydian Augmented #2	1 #2 3 #4 #5 6 7	(W+H) H W W H W H	Maj7(#5)
Locrian bb7	1 b2 b3 4 b5 b6 bb7	H W W H W H (W+H)	Dim7

It is important to have a good grasp of the scale name, intervallic formula and root chord of each of these modes so that you may fully understand the application of the concepts to come. The whole tone/half tone formula is not such an essential category as the other categories within the table (in a practical purpose), but it does not hurt to have an understanding of this as well.

1. Harmonic Major Scale Packs (triad/pentatonic/heptatonic)

Triad

As with both the major and harmonic minor scales, the harmonic major scale deals with just the four basic triads; major, minor, augmented and diminished.

Major	Minor	Augmented	Diminished
1 3 5	1 b3 5	1 3 #5	1 b3 b5

Pentatonic

As with all the other scale pack sections of the book, the pentatonic scale is viewed as a triad with two notes added to it. In the case of the harmonic major scale we begin with a major triad (1 3 5) to which a major 2nd and a b6th are added. The result is the major(b6) pentatonic scale (1 2 3 5 b6).

Triad	2 added notes	Pentatonic Scale
1 3 5	+ 2, b6	= 1 2 3 5 b6

The same process of pentatonic scale modification explained in the melodic minor section of the book is applied and yet again we find some of the usual subjects like the Min(maj7) pentatonic and the Min7(b5) pentatonic, but we also find some new pentatonic scales in the mix.

Pentatonic Scale	Intervallic Construction
Min(maj7)(#11) Pentatonic	1 b3 #4 5 7
Major(b2) Pentatonic	1 b2 3 5 6
Major(#2, #5) Pentatonic	1 #2 3 #5 6
Diminished Pentatonic	1 b3 4 b5 bb7

Heptatonic

Finally, we add two more notes into the equation to result in the seven notes of a full heptatonic scale; in this case the harmonic major scale. To be a bit more specific, the pentatonic base is the major(b6) pentatonic to which we add a 4th and 7th to result in the full intervallic construction of the scale 1 2 3 4 5 b6 7.

Pentatonic Scale	2 added notes	Harmonic Major Scale
1 2 3 5 b6	+ 4, 7	= 1 2 3 4 5 b6 7

Triad > Pentatonic Scale > Heptatonic Scale

Triad	Pentatonic Scale	Heptatonic Scale
Major 1 3 5	Major(b6) 1 2 3 5 b6	Hamonic Major 1 2 3 4 5 b6 7
Diminished 1 b3 b5	Min7(b5) 1 b3 4 b5 b7	Dorian b5 1 2 b3 4 b5 6 b7
Major 1 3 5	Major(b2, b6) 1 b2 3 5 b6	Phrygian b4 1 b2 b3 b4 5 b6 b7
Minor 1 b3 5	Min(maj7)(#11) 1 b3 #4 5 7	Lydian b3 1 2 b3 #4 5 6 7
Major 1 3 5	Major(b2) 1 b2 3 5 6	Mixolydian b2 1 b2 3 4 5 6 b7
Augmented 1 3 #5	Major (#2, #5) 1 #2 3 #5 6	Lydian Augmented #2 1 #2 3 #4 #5 6 7
Diminished 1 b3 b5	Diminished 1 b3 4 b5 bb7	Locrian bb7 1 b2 b3 4 b5 b6 bb7

THE ART OF SCALE WEAVING | 171

Scale Diagrams

Harmonic Major Scale Pack

Major Triad	Major b6 Pentatonic	Harmonic Major
1 3 5	1 2 3 5 b6	1 2 3 4 5 b6 7

Pattern 1

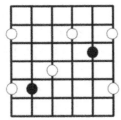 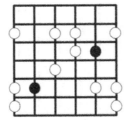 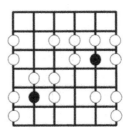

Pattern 2

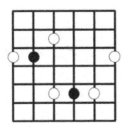 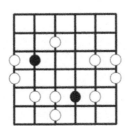 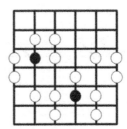

Pattern 3

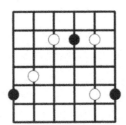 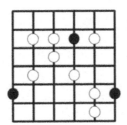 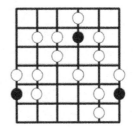

172 | JUAN ANTONIO RIVERA

Pattern 4

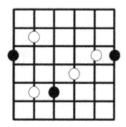 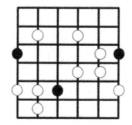 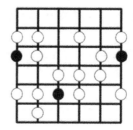

Pattern 5

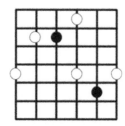 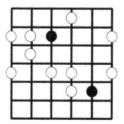 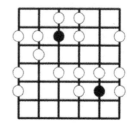

Exercise

F Harmonic Major

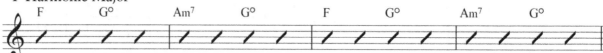

Dorian b5 Scale Pack

Diminished Triad	Min7(b5) Pentatonic	Dorian b5
1 b3 b5	1 b3 4 b5 b7	1 2 b3 4 b5 6 b7

Pattern 1

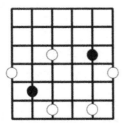 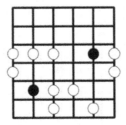 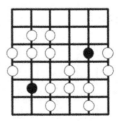

Pattern 2

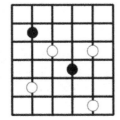 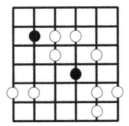 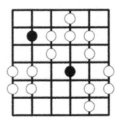

Pattern 3

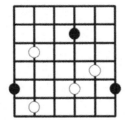 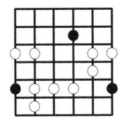 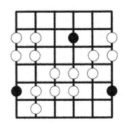

Pattern 4

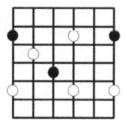 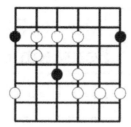 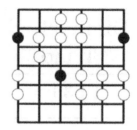

Pattern 5

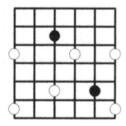 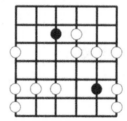 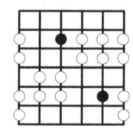

Exercise

Ab Dorian b5

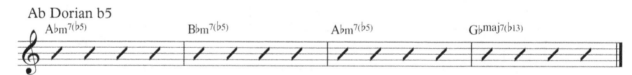

Phrygian b4 Scale Pack

Major Triad	Major (b2, b6) Pentatonic	Phrygian b4
1 3 5	1 b2 3 5 b6	1 b2 b3 b4 5 b6 b7

Pattern 1

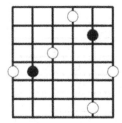 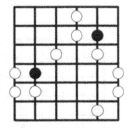 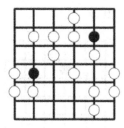

Pattern 2

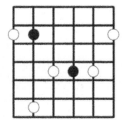 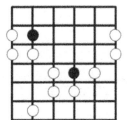 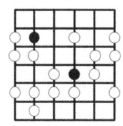

Pattern 3

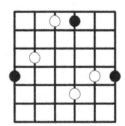 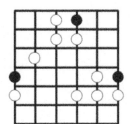 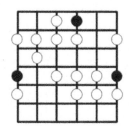

Pattern 4

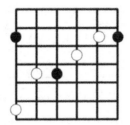 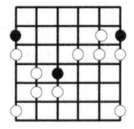 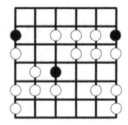

Pattern 5

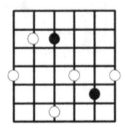 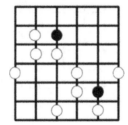 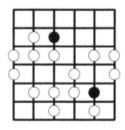

Exercise

Bb Phrygian b4

Lydian b3 Scale Pack

Minor Triad	Min(maj7)(#11) Pentatonic	Lydian b3
1 b3 5	1 b3 #4 5 7	1 2 b3 #4 5 6 7

Pattern 1

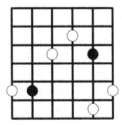 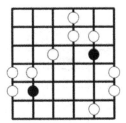 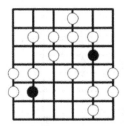

Pattern 2

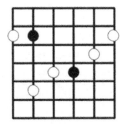 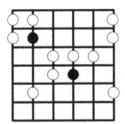 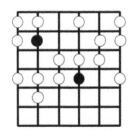

Pattern 3

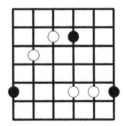 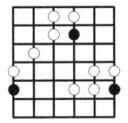 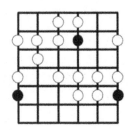

Pattern 4

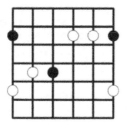 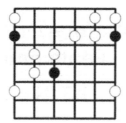 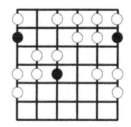

Pattern 5

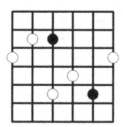 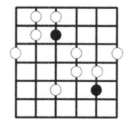 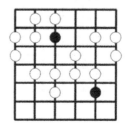

Exercise

D Lydian ♭3

Dm(maj7)   C♯/D   Dm(maj7)   C♯/D

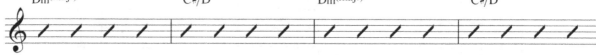

Mixolydian b2 Scale Pack

Major Triad	Major (b2) Pentatonic	Mixolydian b2
1 3 5	1 b2 3 5 6	1 b2 3 4 5 6 b7

Pattern 1

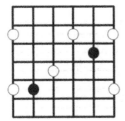 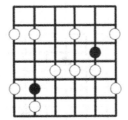 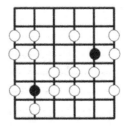

Pattern 2

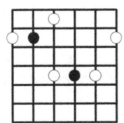 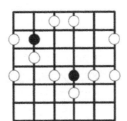 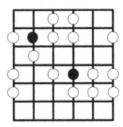

Pattern 3

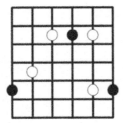 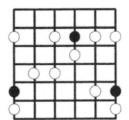 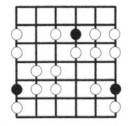

Pattern 4

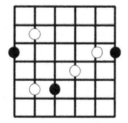 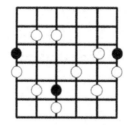 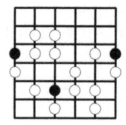

Pattern 5

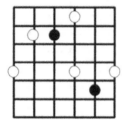 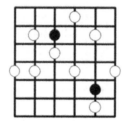 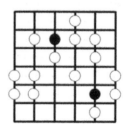

Exercise

C Mixolydian b2

Lydian Augmented #2 Scale Pack

Augmented Triad	Major (#2, #5) Pentatonic	Lydian Augmented #2
1 3 #5	1 #2 3 #5 6	1 #2 3 #4 #5 6 7

Pattern 1

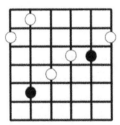 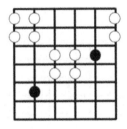 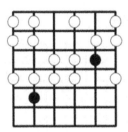

Pattern 2

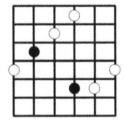 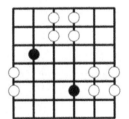 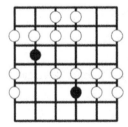

Pattern 3

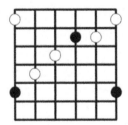 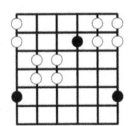 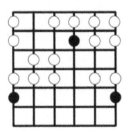

Pattern 4

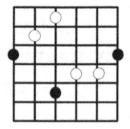 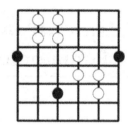 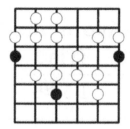

Pattern 5

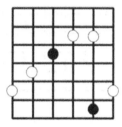 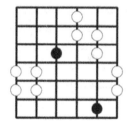 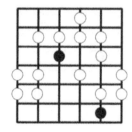

Exercise

A Lydian Augmented #2

Locrian bb7 Scale Pack

Diminished Triad	Diminished Pentatonic	Locrian bb7
1 b3 b5	1 b3 4 b5 bb7	1 b2 b3 4 b5 b6 bb7

Pattern 1

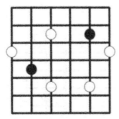 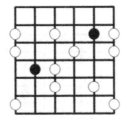 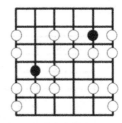

Pattern 2

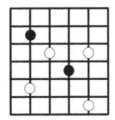 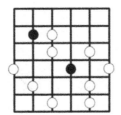 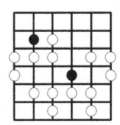

Pattern 3

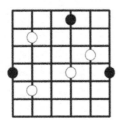 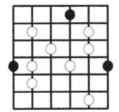 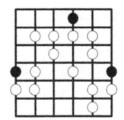

Pattern 4

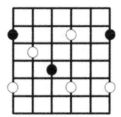 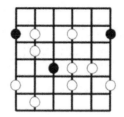 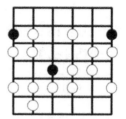

Pattern 5

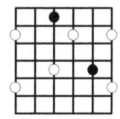 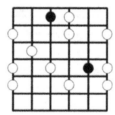 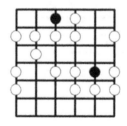

Exercise

C# Locrian bb7

Exercise and Application

- Learn the material

As mentioned in other "exercise and application" sections of the book; it's of absolute importance to learn the material really well. It has to become second nature and part of your common vocabulary. It gets easier to apply the material over more sections of the book once you learn the bases since some of this base material is repeated across all four chapters.

A good example of this repetition (in the scale pack sections of the book), is the use of triads. There are five main triads that are repeated throughout the whole book (major, minor, augmented, diminished and major b5); all you have to do is learn the different applications for these triads once you know them by heart.

- Pick and choose

The harmonic major scale is definitely one to be explored and taken advantage of since at this point not a lot of players out there are using it. It's the perfect scale (along with its modes) to begin developing a personal sound out of.

- Develop a style

Sit down with the triads, pentatonic scales and modes that you prefer and try to work out different ways of application. You can look to mix and match the chords of the harmonic major scale with those of the major, melodic minor and harmonic minor scales. Look for ways that sound the best according to your own ear.

2. Harmonized Scale Weaving

If you have been following the book step by step you are probably getting tired of these introductions since they are very similar in fashion. But I do have to make sure that anyone that has skipped a page or two understands the different sections within the chapters.

If you are part of the group that has been following the book in its order you already know that the harmonized scale refers to the 7 chords that are obtained as a result of stacking 3rds on top of every note within the scale. In this case we are working with the harmonic major scale and as an example I've provided the results of such stacking below.

These results are then standardized to each key by setting the chord qualities next to roman numerals representing each scale degree. Below is a table with exactly that.

Harmonized Harmonic Major Scale						
Imaj7	IIm7(b5)	IIIm7	IVm(maj7)	V7	bVImaj7(#5)	VII°7

The scale diagrams are represented by the use of the harmonized scale weaving system in which the notes of the 7th arpeggios are displayed in grey, their root in black and the remaining scale notes are presented in white.

⬤ 7th Arpeggio

◯ Scale or mode

● Root of the 7th arpeggio

Vertical Harmonized Scale

If you've already studied the harmonized scale of the other chapters (and scales) then you already know how the books system works and you can get on down to the fun stuff in the scale diagrams. If you haven't, then keep reading.

The vertical harmonized scale is displayed by utilizing all five patterns of the CAGED system and laying out the seven arpeggios that stem from each scale degree of the harmonic major scale. For example, take the CAGED system's pattern 1 of the harmonic major scale. That pattern is portrayed at the top of the page while underneath it appears the same pattern of the scale, but on each of the seven diagrams there is a different arpeggio that is built from a different scale degree.

Remember to practice this is in all of the keys of the harmonic major scale.

Scale Diagrams

Vertical Harmonized Harmonic Major Scale (Pattern 1)

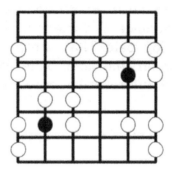

Imaj7   IIm7(b5)   IIIm7   IVm(maj7)

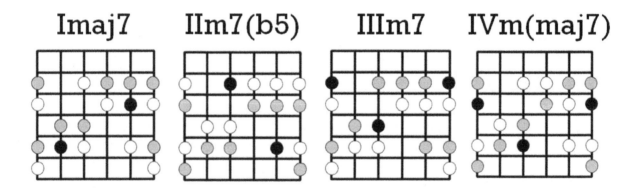

V7   bVImaj7(#5)   VII°7

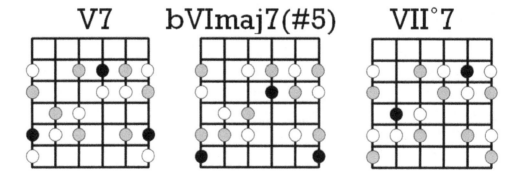

Vertical Harmonized Harmonic Major Scale (Pattern 2)

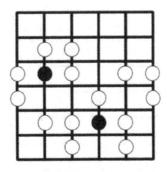

Imaj7   IIm7(b5)   IIIm7   IVm(maj7)

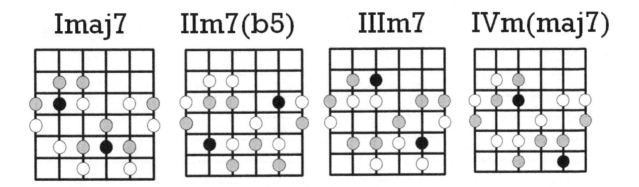

V7   bVImaj7(#5)   VII°7

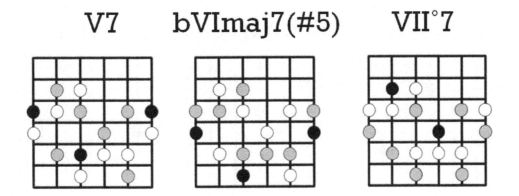

Vertical Harmonized Harmonic Major Scale (Pattern 3)

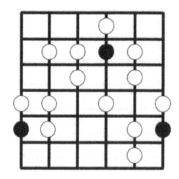

Imaj7   IIm7(b5)   IIIm7   IVm(maj7)

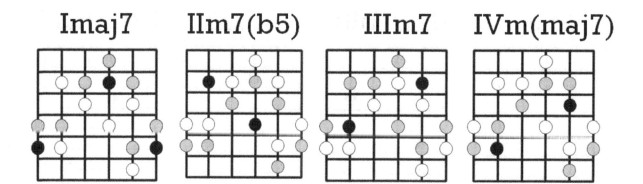

V7   bVImaj7(#5)   VII°7

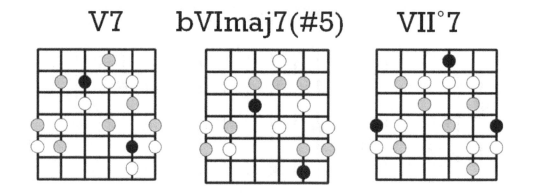

Vertical Harmonized Harmonic Major Scale (Pattern 4)

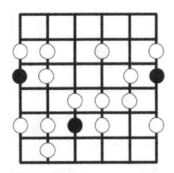

Imaj7   IIm7(b5)   IIIm7   IVm(maj7)

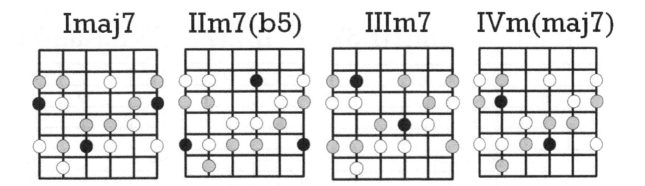

V7   bVImaj7(#5)   VII°7

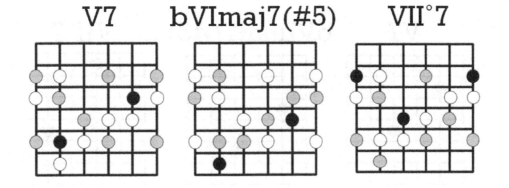

Vertical Harmonized Harmonic Major Scale (Pattern 5)

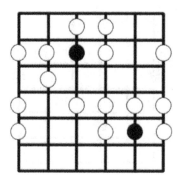

Imaj7   IIm7(b5)   IIIm7   IVm(maj7)

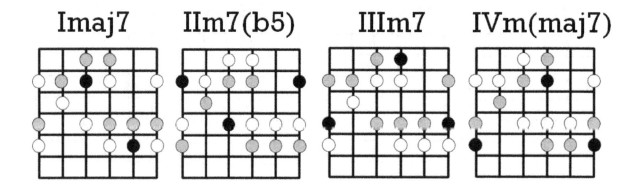

V7   bVImaj7(#5)   VII°7

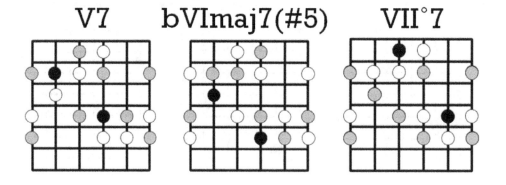

Exercise and Application

- Learn the harmonized scale order

Learn all five CAGED scale patterns with their seven respective arpeggios in their order. Play the Imaj7 arpeggio, followed by the IIm7(b5), then the IIIm7 and so on until you reach the octave. You can use a metronome once familiarized with the patterns to create fluidity and cleanness.

- Practice shifting between specific arpeggios and the scale

You can practice each arpeggio on their own and how they feel as you shift between the scale and that one specific arpeggio. It's important to get to know the feel, look and sound of each arpeggio within the scale in order to achieve fluidity in performance. This is to be repeated on all five positions of the CAGED system and all seven of the arpeggios of the scale.

Also practice shifting between the seven arpeggios and the notes of the scale.

- Practice weaving the harmonized harmonic major scale with other scales

As with the harmonic and melodic minor scales, the harmonic major scale is used as a spice; adding bits and pieces here and there. It's important to practice going in and out of the harmonic major scale along with the major scale, melodic minor scale and the harmonic minor scale.

- Practice over Jazz Standards and other tunes

Apply the arpeggios and scale over your favorite jazz standards and other tunes to add a more practical practicing approach of the material. Follow the chords of the tunes with just the arpeggios over one of the CAGED scale patterns. You can also practice flowing/shifting between the arpeggios and scales over the same tunes.

This is to be repeated over all five patterns of the CAGED system.

It is also important to mix up the harmonized harmonic major scale with other scales (especially the major scale) when practicing over tunes.

- Write your own tunes

Being that this is one of the least used scales in the book you can definitely build upon it to create a unique sound. What better way of doing this than by writing new music around it.

Horizontal Harmonized Scale

As with the vertical harmonized scale, if you are already familiarized with how the system works you can head down to the fun stuff. If not, then keep on reading.

To understand the horizontal harmonized harmonic major scale you have to be able to play the scale on just one string.

For example, take the notes in C harmonic major. Let's work on playing that scale up the 5th string. It would look something like this.

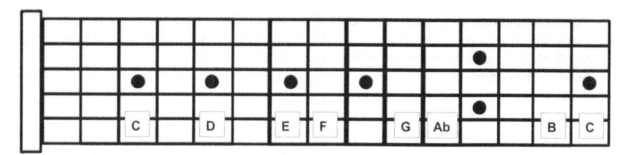

Once having visualized the scale over one string in a horizontal fashion, the next step is to visualize and practice the positioning of both the harmonic major and the seven arpeggios that stem from that scale.

Another way to look at it (in this case), is by starting from the C in the 3rd fret and playing both the arpeggio of the Imaj7 chord (using the pattern 1 octave of the CAGED system) and the harmonic minor scale pattern over which that arpeggio appears. Next go to the D note in the 5th fret and play both the arpeggio of the IIm7(b5) chord (using the pattern 1 octave of the CAGED system) and the harmonic major scale pattern over which that arpeggio appears. Then keep repeating this process until you complete the scale by reaching the C note at the 15th fret.

This process is to be repeated on all five octaves of the CAGED system, all six strings of the instrument and all twelve keys of the harmonic major scale.

Scale Diagrams

Horizontal Harmonized Harmonic Major Scale (Pattern 1)

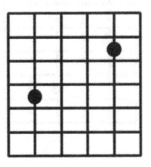

Imaj7 IIm7(b5) IIIm7 IVm(maj7)

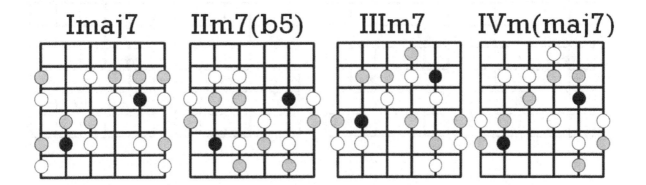

V7 bVImaj7(#5) VII°7

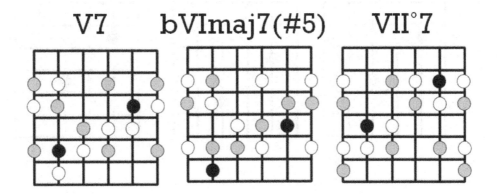

Horizontal Harmonized Harmonic Major Scale (Pattern 2)

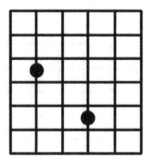

Imaj7   IIm7(b5)   IIIm7   IVm(maj7)

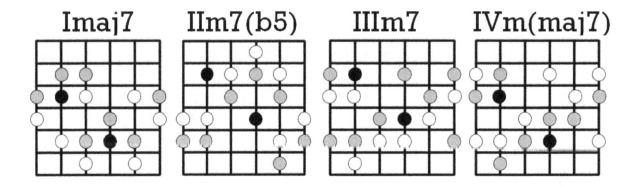

V7   bVImaj7(#5)   VII°7

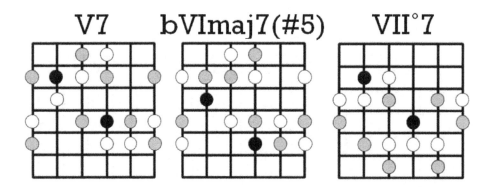

Horizontal Harmonized Harmonic Major Scale (Pattern 3)

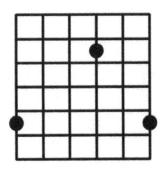

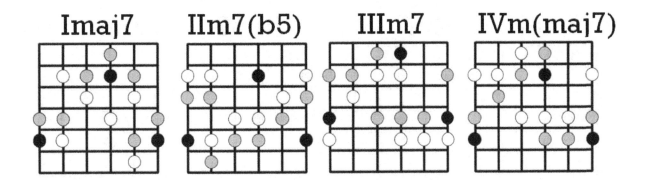

Imaj7   IIm7(b5)   IIIm7   IVm(maj7)

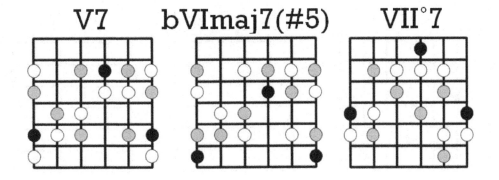

V7   bVImaj7(#5)   VII°7

Horizontal Harmonized Harmonic Major Scale (Pattern 4)

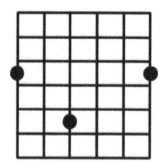

Imaj7 IIm7(b5) IIIm7 IVm(maj7)

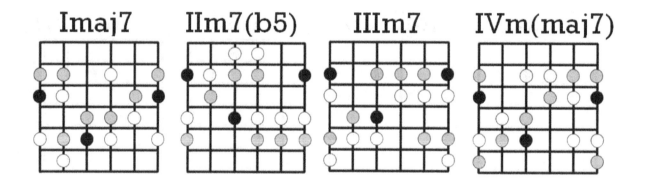

V7 bVImaj7(#5) VII°7

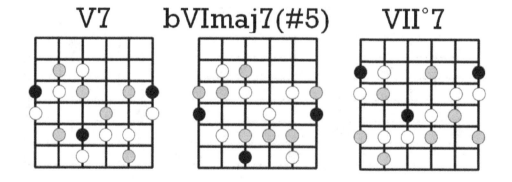

Horizontal Harmonized Harmonic Major Scale (Pattern 5)

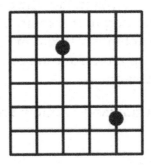

Imaj7   IIm7(b5)   IIIm7   IVm(maj7)

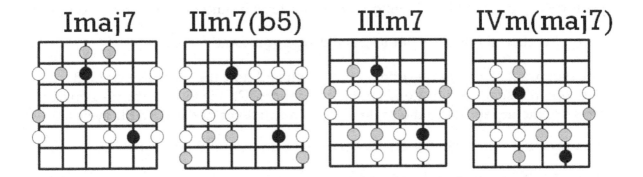

V7   bVImaj7(#5)   VII°7

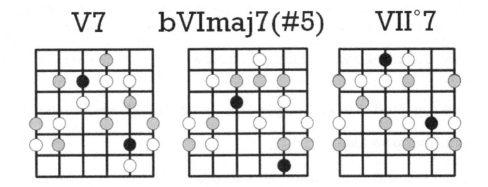

Exercise and Application

- Learn the harmonized scale order

Learn all seven arpeggios in order over the same string root. Play the Imaj7 arpeggio, followed by the IIm7(b5), then the IIIm7 and so on until you reach the octave. This time you will be sticking to the same CAGED octave for the arpeggios. This means that the actual scale patterns will be shifting on just about every new arpeggio. You can use a metronome once familiarized with the patterns to create fluidity and cleanness.

- Practice weaving the harmonized harmonic major scale along with other scales

The ability to change between different scales and arpeggios mid solo will heavily influence your sound, note choices and confidence when it comes to performing. It also aids in having a better understanding of music in the long run.

- Practice shifting between specific arpeggios and the scale

You can practice each arpeggio on their own and how they feel as you shift between the scale and that one specific arpeggio. This is to be repeated on all seven of the arpeggios of the scale and all five octaves of the CAGED system.

Also practice shifting between the seven arpeggios and the notes of the scale.

- Practice over Jazz Standards and other tunes

Apply the arpeggios and scale over your favorite jazz standards and/or any other tune to add a more practical approach of the material. Follow the chords of the tunes with just the arpeggios over one of the strings on the guitar.

You can also practice flowing/shifting between the arpeggios and scales over the same tunes.

This is to be repeated over all five patterns of the CAGED scale patterns.

- Write your own tunes

Write some tunes and songs based around this scale, its arpeggios and the rest of the other scales that you have already studied in the book. I'm sure that you will find some new and interesting sounds from this material.

3. Pentatonic Scale Weaving

Last but not least, the pentatonic scale weaving section of the book for the harmonic major scale. As I've already mentioned, the harmonic major scale has lot to offer when looking for new colors and textures that are not common among guitar players; take advantage of this (this includes the pentatonic scales within it).

The process to attain these pentatonic scales is the same as with the other pentatonic weaving sections in the book.

As with the other pentatonic weaving sections, the notes of the pentatonic scale are depicted in grey while the rest of the heptatonic scale is depicted in white. The root of both of these scales is depicted as black.

◯ Pentatonic scale

◯ Scale or mode

● Root of the scale

Pentatonic Scale > Heptatonic Scale

Modal Order	Pentatonic Scale	Heptatonic Scale
1	Major(b6) 1 2 3 5 b6	Hamonic Major 1 2 3 4 5 b6 7
2	Min7(b5) 1 b3 4 b5 b7	Dorian b5 1 2 b3 4 b5 6 b7
3	Major(b2, b6) 1 b2 3 5 b6	Phrygian b4 1 b2 b3 b4 5 b6 b7
4	Min(maj7)(#11) 1 b3 #4 5 7	Lydian b3 1 2 b3 #4 5 6 7
5	Major(b2) 1 b2 3 5 6	Mixolydian b2 1 b2 3 4 5 6 b7
6	Major (#2, #5) 1 #2 3 #5 6	Lydian Augmented #2 1 #2 3 #4 #5 6 7
7	Diminished 1 b3 4 b5 bb7	Locrian bb7 1 b2 b3 4 b5 b6 bb7

Scale Diagrams

Harmonic Major w/ Major (b6) Pentatonic Weaving

Major (b6) Pentatonic	Harmonic Major
1 2 3 5 b6	1 2 3 4 5 b6 7

- **Chords to play over: Major, Maj7, Maj9, Maj7(b13), etc.**

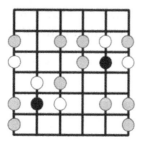 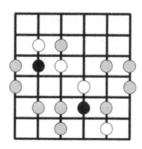 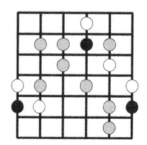

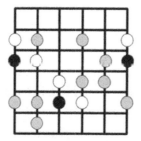 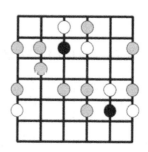

Exercise

A Harmonic Major

Dorian b5 w/ Min7(b5) Pentatonic Weaving

Min7(b5) Pentatonic	Dorian b5
1 b3 4 b5 b7	1 2 b3 4 b5 6 b7

- **Chords to play over: Diminished triad, Min7(b5), Min9(b5), Min13(b5), etc.**

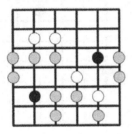 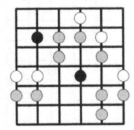 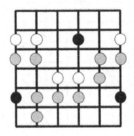

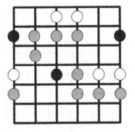 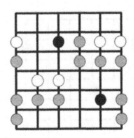

Exercise

D Dorian b5

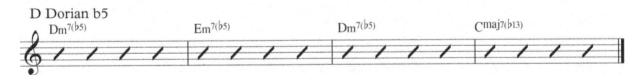

Phrygian b4 w/ Major (b2, b6) Pentatonic Weaving

Major (b2, b6) Pentatonic	Phrygian b4
1 b2 3 5 b6	1 b2 b3 b4 5 b6 b7 1 b2 #2 3 5 b6 b7

- **Chords to play over: Minor, Major, Min7, Dom7, Dom7(alt), etc.**

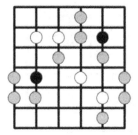 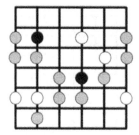 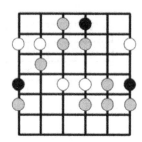

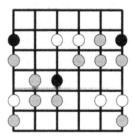 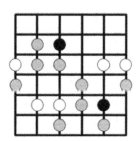

Exercise

F# Phrygian b4

Lydian b3 w/ Min(maj7) Pentatonic Weaving

Min(maj7)(#11) Pentatonic	Lydian b3
1 b3 #4 5 7	1 2 b3 #4 5 6 7

- **Chords to play over: Minor, Min(maj7), Min(maj9), Min(maj7)(#11), Min(maj13), etc.**

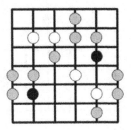 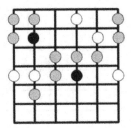 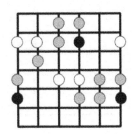

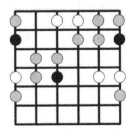 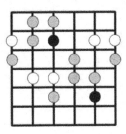

Exercise

C Lydian b3

Cm(maj7)   B/C   Cm(maj7)   B/C

Mixolydian b2 w/ Major(b2) Pentatonic Weaving

Major (b2) Pentatonic	Mixolydian b2
1 b2 3 5 6	1 b2 3 4 5 6 b7

- **Chords to play over: Major, Dom7, Dom7(b9), Dom11, Dom13, etc.**

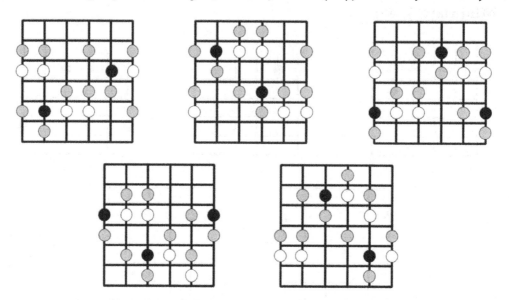

Exercise

Bb Mixolydian b2

Lydian Augmented #2 w/ Major (#2) Pentatonic Weaving

Major (#2) Pentatonic	Lydian Augmented #2
1 #2 3 #5 6	1 #2 3 #4 #5 6 7

- **Chords to play over: Major, Major7(#5), Major7(#5, #11), etc.**

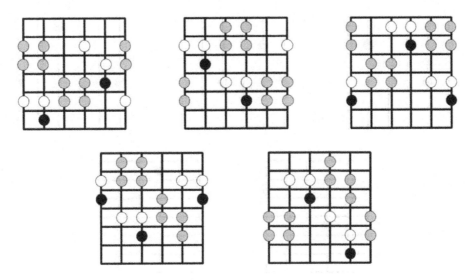

Exercise

F Lydian Augmented #2

Locrian bb7 w/ Diminished Pentatonic Weaving

Diminished Pentatonic	Locrian bb7
1 b3 4 b5 bb7	1 b2 b3 4 b5 b6 bb7

- **Chords to play over: Diminished triad, Dim7**

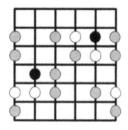 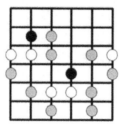 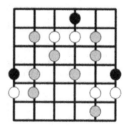

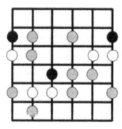 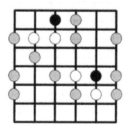

Exercise

E Locrian bb7

Exercise and Application

- **Learn the material**

Make sure to know your material from top to bottom. The better you know the material and the more you practice its application the better you will sound when you play. Memorize, learn and apply the material in as many ways as possible.

- **Practice going in and out**

The harmonic major scale is a great aid in spicing up your sound when soloing and composing. Subtle use of this scale will add depth and intrigue into your music. To do this on the fly you need to have the ability to go into the scale (and modes) and head back out to your main tonality.

- **Write music!**

I know, I know, I just keep repeating this but it is absolutely imperative that you write music with this information. The whole point behind this material is in the creation of good music. No better moment to start writing your music than right now so get to it!

Closing Words

I have used the concepts in this book on my own journey, have helped others on their way with these ideas and have seen countless others musicians prosper as their musical perspective widens through the lens of connection. And that's the main idea behind this book; connection. If you get anything from this book it should be the idea that everything in music is related. Arpeggios, triads, chords, scales, pentatonic scales, etc. they are all related in one way of another. It's our responsibility as musicians to study these relationships and to best judge which ones resonate with our own artistic vision.

With this, you should also look into taking the information in this book and making it yours. Learn it, apply it, customize it, do what you want with it but make it yours. Get creative with it; look for new ways to apply what you already know and whatever you learn from this book. Know that these are only but a few building blocks to start from. You have to take what is of most use to you and leave out the rest to create your own voice. The whole point of learning new material is so that you may apply it to what YOU do.

I am confident that with the proper vision and work ethic you can achieve anything you want.

Good luck!

About the Author

Born in 1989, Juan Antonio grew up in Puerto Rico and has been playing guitar since the age of twelve. While his early influences were rock and blues musicians, he started leaning towards jazz fusion and experimental music during his late teen years.

As soon as he finished high school, he enrolled at Musicians Institute in Los Angeles where he graduated from an Associate's Degree.

While living at L.A., Juan Antonio studied with various guitarists such as Alex Machacek, Greg Howe and Scott Henderson. Here a whole new world of exploration was opened and he jumped in head first into the world of fusion and experimental music.

After graduating, Juan Antonio moved back to Puerto Rico, where he finished a BA in Marketing and has been featured in many radio and TV sessions, as well as several recordings.

Juan Antonio currently resides in Puerto Rico where he teaches at the Caribbean Conservatory of the Arts, an institution that is part of the Berklee International Network.

Made in the USA
Coppell, TX
18 August 2024

36087525R00129